Welcome Baby

31 Easy-to-Make Patchwork and Appliqué
Projects for Infants and Toddlers

Jill Jarnow and Betsy Potter

illustrations by Jill Jarnow
photographs by Jill A. Obrig

CHARLES SCRIBNER'S SONS
New York

Copyright © 1986 Jill Jarnow

Library of Congress Cataloging-in-Publication Data

Jarnow, Jill.
Welcome baby.

1. Patchwork—Patterns. 2. Appliqué—Patterns.
3. Infants—Clothing. 4. Children's clothing.
I. Potter, Betsy. II. Title.
TT835.J373 1986 746.9′2 85-26213
ISBN-0-684-18397-8

1 3 5 7 9 11 13 15 17 19 F/C 20 18 16 14 12 10 8 6 4 2

Printed in the United States of America.

Welcome Baby

For our children with love—Daniel Potter, Liza Potter, and Jesse Jarnow

Contents

Acknowledgments

Many, many thanks to Amy Berkower and Susan Cohen, whose determination caused this book to be conceived, and to Maron Waxman, whose hard work allowed this book to be born.

And special thanks to our family and friends for their enthusiasm and help—to Lani Hee and Ann Gardiner for their spectacular sewing; to Jackie Fisher for her wonderful calligraphy design; to Jill Obrig for her fabulous photography and quilt; to Sara, B.D., Nicholas, Alicia, and Benjamin Colen for letting us invade their beautiful house with lights, cameras, and sewing projects; and to our husbands and children, who probably wondered how two grown women could get so excited about little pieces of fabric.

Welcome
Baby

Introduction

After spending hours admiring the fabulous patchwork, appliqué, and quilted baby items with their big price tags in needlework and children's shops from Madison Avenue to Rodeo Drive, we decided to go home and create quilts and accessories for our own families. We were sure we could do it easily and a lot less expensively.

Experimenting as we went, we stitched tote bags, wall hangings, quilts, toys, washcloths, and pillows. In the process we made one very important discovery: The success of any sewing project depends more on the choice and arrangement of the colors and fabrics than on the intricacy of the needlework itself.

This is the idea behind *Welcome Baby*. Take it to heart, and we're sure that you'll soon see a tremendous difference in your finished projects, whether you are making just one quilt for that special baby in your life or whether you sew all the time.

FOCUS ON FABRIC

Spend your time choosing and arranging your materials into combinations that are exciting to look at, and everything else will fall into place. Of course, using great colors cannot make up for sloppy workmanship. You should make your sewing as neat as possible. Not only does poor stitching detract from the overall effect of your finished project, but it also comes apart quickly.

You needn't have been trained in the French couture to enjoy making the projects in *Welcome Baby*. We intend them to be easy yet enticing enough for people at all levels of sewing accomplishment.

SEWING—HAND VERSUS MACHINE

Do we recommend sewing by hand or machine? Each has its own benefits. Betsy, the quiltaholic of our team, prefers to piece together her quilt tops by machine because machine stitching is faster and stronger. Jill, on the other hand, loves nothing better than sitting peacefully making hand stitches. Betsy has, by this time, convinced Jill that machine stitching is best for quilt-top assembly, but we both agree that there is no substitute for hand quilting.

As for appliqué, we're each holding out for our personal preferences, and you'll have to draw your own conclusions according to what you like to do. Some of our projects, such as the Scotty Quilt on page 103, are machine appliquéd. Others, such as the I-Can-Do-It Book on page 109, are hand stitched. Guess who stitched which! When making any of these projects, use the technique you like best.

POSSIBILITIES AND OPTIONS

Welcome Baby is filled with small, portable, quick-to-complete projects to make for babies, but the possibilities for variation are endless.

The Scotty Quilt is a good example. We chose small plaids for our Scotties because that was the mood we were in that day. The little dogs would look equally terrific cut from gingham, pin-dot, floral, or solid-color cotton. We used plaid bows to decorate their necks because they appealed to us at the moment we were planning the quilt. But we know that solid, dotted, or striped ribbon would also have been fun. Choose materials for your projects according to what appeals to

you. The most important factor is your own taste.

After you have completed one or two baby quilts, you may want to go on to bigger things. We're happy to tell you that the stitchery process is the same for any size quilt. Use the Scotty or any other motif in this book. Just buy larger amounts of fabric, measure carefully, and make more or bigger quilt squares.

THE CREATIVE YOU

We want to stress here that we think of *Welcome Baby* as a book filled with ideas and guidelines to mix and match. Even though it's a book of specific projects, we want you to use our suggestions as stepping-stones toward expressing your own tastes and ideas.

A lot of people we run into insist that they aren't creative and feel more comfortable following instructions. But one activity doesn't have to exclude the other. When you assemble materials to make any of our projects, you'll find yourself reinterpreting our colors and prints either because your local shop doesn't have exactly what we used or because you simply prefer another fabric or color combination. If you hold out for fabrics that you love and arrange and rearrange them into combinations that really sing to you, we know you'll be thrilled with your finished project. And this, whether or not you want to admit it to yourself, is the result of your creativity.

As you gain experience and confidence, we hope you will borrow ideas and color combinations that appeal to you from all over—books, magazines, museums, swatches of fabric, or even the sewing projects of your friends. That's what inspiration is about.

WHY WELCOME BABY

Finally, in a world overflowing with impersonal plastics, we want the projects in *Welcome Baby* to add warmth and security to the environment of babies. We hope that you will find our collection and our encouragement just what you need to create wonderful patchwork, appliqué and quilted accessories, and toys to be enjoyed by new arrivals and their families for years to come.

All we ask, when you give your gift to its lucky recipient, is that you say proudly, "I made it myself."

Jill Jarnow
Betsy Potter

Fabrics

Choosing fabric is the most important part of any project in this book, so take your time making your purchases and decisions even if you have to visit two or three shops to find what you want. If you settle for materials that are not quite to your taste, you will miss the pleasure of knowing you created your project without compromise.

Cost may also be a consideration, but again in many cases you'll find it worthwhile to spend a little extra to get a print or color that you love. In the long run, the extra time and money you spend choosing fabrics will pay off because you'll be happy with the patchwork that you've created.

There are other benefits to buying what you like. Carefully chosen and arranged fabrics can overshadow many imperfections in sewing techniques as well as most of the weaknesses you might have as an inexperienced craftsperson. If you are a beginner, this can be very encouraging.

The following sections include hints to help you choose fabrics and colors. We can't tell you what colors to choose, and we certainly don't advocate copying the colors in our projects exactly. Instead, we want to encourage you to select what is most fitting to your tastes and needs.

FIBER CONTENT

It would be great if all the beautiful printed cotton in yard goods stores was really cotton, but most often it is a cotton/polyester blend, which works just fine. We do advise you to avoid 100 percent polyester fabrics because they are difficult to use, they pill after several washings, and they hold stains that would wash out of other fabrics. On the other hand, if you try to use 100 percent cotton to the exclusion of all else, you'll miss out on a lot of great prints.

Fiber content will also affect the look of your finished quilt. After a few washings, 100 percent cotton will produce a traditional, well-used appearance. For this reason, we both like using unbleached muslin. It sews well, ages beautifully, and has a traditional look. We try to use it as often as possible. Polyester/cotton fabric, on the other hand, will retain a bright, more contemporary look. If the difference is important to you, choose your fabrics accordingly. Our advice is to check the fiber content of fabrics, which is usually printed on the cardboard bolt, and where possible, select materials that are at least 50 percent cotton.

FABRIC WEIGHT

Try to choose fabrics of equal weight and texture for your patchwork. However, if you fall in love with a print of slightly heavier material, such as kettle cloth, be assured that you won't ruin your project by using it.

COLOR SCHEMES

The colors you choose for your patchwork will be the major factor in determining the overall look of your finished project. Please notice the three Star Quilts in the color pictures that begin on page 57. Each pattern is identical, but we have made them look very different by varying our color combinations. You can turn a simple patchwork pattern or a primitive appliqué into a stimulating piece of needlework by choosing fabrics in colors and patterns that complement one another.

Choosing Colors You'll Enjoy

If you are making a quilt to be used in a specific area such as a baby's room, playroom, or living room, you may want to choose an item in that room—the wallpaper or even a picture—to use as a guide when selecting colors. If you are making a quilt for someone else, be sure to consider the decorating tastes and color schemes of that person when deciding on fabrics.

When practical, bring a swatch of wallpaper, a picture, or even a piece of material to the yard goods shop to use as a color reference when you buy fabrics. Choose whatever catches your eye in those colors and lay the bolts of material out on a counter. Arrange them in various combinations until you decide what looks best.

If you are feeling overwhelmed by the number of possibilities, we are happy to report that most shops are staffed by knowledgeable and capable people who are usually more than delighted to offer advice.

Be Daring

It's sometimes a lot more fun to let practicality fall by the wayside and choose offbeat color schemes merely because they satisfy your aesthetic instincts. One of the most exciting quilts we have ever seen was a combination of purple, orange, gray, and red prints. An unusual mixture, to be sure, but because of the way the colors had been chosen and arranged, the overall effect was spectacular.

Solids and Prints

You will have a lot of fun if you use an assortment of small prints in your patchwork, and you will also create a warm, friendly look that children enjoy. We love to mix tiny printed fabrics. But solid-color fabrics make beautiful patchwork as well, and you may want to consider using them if they are to your taste.

If you are nervous about combining a lot of prints, we suggest mixing small prints with geometric patterns such as pindots, ginghams, stripes, or plaids. Pindots are available in a wide variety of colors and look great with almost any print. Avoid using large prints or patterns for your small patchwork pieces because they tend to be overwhelming and the print usually gets lost.

THEME FABRICS

The market is constantly changing, but from time to time you may see printed picture panels, stencils, or commercial patterns that appeal to you. Examples of these fabrics would be storybook characters, country-look stencils, or cartoon figures. Many tend to be trite or corny, so please use discretion when using these fabrics.

Choose something with a classic look worthy of your time and effort.

LEFTOVERS

Keep scraps left over from your sewing projects. Very often you'll find that the small piece of yardage you set aside last year is just what you need for a project in this book. (The stuffed Scotty Dog on page 106 was made from leftovers from the Scotty Quilt.)

Scraps are fun to use, and you can often evoke wonderful memories by using a favorite article of clothing or household accessory. If you use old clothing scraps in your projects, make sure that they are still strong, fresh, and in good condition. For more, turn to page 7, Sewing with Scraps.

COLLECTING FABRICS

Collecting fabrics in wonderful prints and colors is our favorite part of quilt-making, except, of course, admiring our finished quilts. If *Welcome Baby* is your first sewing experience, you will probably buy fabrics in the exact amounts that you need for your chosen project.

We can't rave enough about the pleasures of collecting fabrics for that proverbial rainy day. It's so satisfying and often inspiring to know that at any time you could pull out your materials and get to work.

The first way to start a collection is to let it happen by itself. Once you complete your first sewing project, you will have leftovers. Store them away in a closet or drawer; that's the beginning of your fabric collection.

If you are a serious quiltmaker, consider buying cuts of fabric when you see something you like in the store. The great fun of patchwork is to create warm textures by combining prints. In most cases, ¼ yard is all you will need in a patchwork quilt top, and if you have great fabrics on hand, you'll find yourself doing a lot more sewing. When your collection gets large enough, store and sort your scraps and leftover fabrics by color to help you keep track of your selection.

THOUGHTS ON FABRIC SHOPPING

We *love* to shop for fabric. It's so much fun to discover great colors and patterns and arrange them into even more wonderful combinations. Because there are a number of different types of fabric shops in our neighborhoods—Betsy's in California, Jill's in New York—we have found that we patronize them all at different times for different reasons. And when one of us visits the other, the first thing we do is go exploring for fabric.

Stores that specialize in fabric, appliqué, and quilting supplies are scattered throughout the country. Crazy Ladies and Friends, in Santa Monica, California, is run by Mary Ellen Hopkins, and it is one of our favorites. Mary Ellen's enthusiasm and her shop walls plastered with quilts in all stages of completion make you want to rush home to start quilting.

However, we can't overlook the fact that there are other fabric shops in the world. Some of them may be closer to your home, some may have just the print you are looking for, and some may have bargain prices. Variety stores, department stores, all-purpose fabric stores, and chain fabric stores are out there waiting to be explored.

If we are working on a special project and have time to check out all the possibilities, we will. When we planned the Scotty Quilt, we visited three different shops before we had the assortment of plaids we wanted. It was so much fun!

Of course, there are times when neither of us has had a spare second. When this is your situation, we suggest you head for a conveniently located shop that you think will have what you want. But if you are looking for something very specific, such as red and white fabric, and what they have in stock just isn't quite what you had in mind, take some extra time in the near future to continue your search. Finding what you like is worth the effort.

SEWING WITH SCRAPS

We don't want to overlook our readers who live miles from a fabric store or who simply cannot afford to purchase fabrics. Let us assure you that you can make wonderful patchwork, appliqué, and quilted projects using scrap bag materials. Sewing for babies is especially easy with scraps because you need only small amounts. And cotton fabrics from worn garments have an aged patina that adds a special touch of warmth to patchwork and appliqué.

But good scrap bags take time to develop, so start collecting outgrown and worn-out cotton clothing as soon as you can. Ask people you know to set aside clothes that have become unwearable.

Before beginning a sewing project, wash and dry the garments in your collection and examine them carefully under a good light. Cut away and save only the fabric that is still strong and unblemished. A shirt with worn-out elbows will have sections that are still in fine condition, and these are the pieces to save for sewing. Fabrics that are weak and stained wear out so quickly that your stitchery efforts will deteriorate after very little use.

MAIL ORDER

If you can afford to buy fabric but you live away from convenient shopping, you can order all the supplies you need through the mail. But because we feel that combining fabrics artistically is such an important part of patchwork and appliqué, we would recommend that you consider using good quality scraps as described in the previous section rather than depend on a catalog photograph for making decisions.

We have found the following firms to be reliable:

Herrschners, Inc., Stevens Point, Wisconsin 54481

J. C. Penney Company, Inc., Catalog Division, Box 1270, Milwaukee, Wisconsin 53201

Lee Wards, 840 North State Street, Elgin, Illinois 60120

Sears, Roebuck and Co., Dept. 139A, 2650 E. Olympic Blvd., Los Angeles, California 90051

COMBINING OLD AND NEW FABRIC

You can combine fabric from old, well-loved pieces of cotton-blend clothing with new materials and get great results if you take a few important precautions.

First, wash all used material before you begin and double-check that it is still strong, as discussed in the section on Sewing with Scraps. Second, make sure to wash all the new materials as well, several times if necessary, to help them take on that worn look that will blend with the scrap materials. The underlying concept of patchwork is that we combine many pieces of unrelated fabric to create a new, unified, and beautiful whole. While it's especially rewarding to spot old fabrics in a new quilt, it's very disconcerting to look at the quilt and have the colors of the new fabric jump out at you. With a little extra washing, you can eliminate this problem.

Supplies

Patchwork, appliqué, and quilting can be incredibly enjoyable and satisfying and even addictive if you have all your tools and materials assembled and provide yourself with a clear, flat work space and good light. Most of the materials in the list that follows are inexpensive, and you'll be able to find them easily in a variety or yard goods shop. If, however, you are a beginner, we don't suggest that you run out and invest your life savings before you even get started. Consider borrowing the bigger items for your first project. Inferior tools are a poor investment, and they may even hinder your enjoyment of quiltmaking. So where price is in question, look for good value, rather than the cheapest or most expensive.

Scissors

Large good cutting scissors are vital to successful and happy sewing. You shouldn't have to spend more than ten dollars for a good pair. Ask for help at your local yard goods store.

Needles

You will need an assortment of needles for hand sewing, embroidery, and your sewing machine. For felt, you will need a sharp crewel needle.

Pins

For ease in handling, buy a box of pins with colored-glass or plastic heads. Discard any that become bent or rusted.

Thread

Keep on hand thread in an assortment of colors for hand stitching, machine sewing, and quilting. If you have an established thread supply, you will find yourself more likely to start a project on a rainy day or quiet evening.

Although cotton thread is easiest to use, it is also hard to find. Cotton-covered polyester thread is fine, but we do *not* recommend 100 percent polyester thread because it tangles and breaks easily.

Quilting thread is available in most yard goods stores. It is a thicker cotton thread with a waxed surface for easy stitching through layers of a quilt. White or off-white are good colors for all projects.

If you become serious about stitchery, you might also want to start a small collection of embroidery thread and floss in different colors and weights.

As you do more and more patchwork, you'll find yourself running through vast quantities of thread. We suggest you stock up on gray and beige thread for all seam sewing. It will simplify your life, and no one will ever know what color you used to stitch together your multicolored quilt.

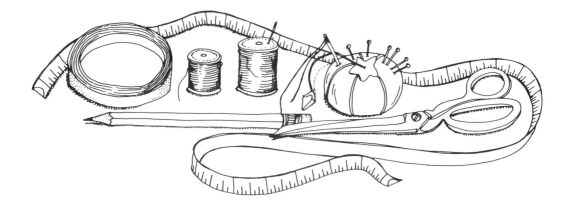

For top stitching, machine zigzagging, or any other stitching that shows, we recommend that you stick to a thread color that blends with or enhances the fabric.

Ruler and Tape Measure

A ruler and a 60-inch tape measure are also indispensable when sewing the projects in this book.

Seam Ripper

We hope that you never have to use a seam ripper, but just in case, it makes it a lot easier to remove stitches from where they weren't meant to be. It can slip into small machine stitches more easily and safely than a scissors.

Cardboard

When you get a new shirt or set of sheets, be sure to set aside the card-board enclosed for your patchwork templates. You can also buy cardboard in art supply stores.

Pencil and Pen

Use either a pencil or ballpoint pen for tracing your templates on fabric. Try to resist using felt tip markers since their ink runs when dampened, washed, or ironed with steam.

Iron and Ironing Board

An iron is an absolute *must* for successful patchwork, and an ironing board makes the job a lot easier. (For more on ironing, see page 17.)

Thimble

A thimble is an optional tool that can prevent you from injuring your fingers while hand sewing. Some people love them; others hate them.

Sewing Machine

We did most of the projects in this book with a sewing machine. Although you can use hand sewing for most of them, we suggest you use a machine for assembling patchwork pieces. Not only is it faster; it's also stronger. For quilting, however, we overwhelmingly recommend hand stitching. For more about this, see the Quilting section that begins on page 27.

Good Light

A good lamp will make working a pleasure at any time of day or night. If you have a permanent work space, consider investing in a gooseneck lamp, available in art supply stores. Or you may prefer a conveniently movable standing floor pharmacy lamp, available in home-furnishing stores.

Work Space

Whether you are lucky enough to have a permanent area of your own or whether you borrow a spot on the floor for the time you work, you will need a clear, flat area for marking, cutting, and laying out your project while it is in progress. Of course, a large table is ideal, but a floor or bed is also fine.

Pinking Shears

For felt projects and ravel-free seams, good-quality pinking shears are a great help. Don't waste your money

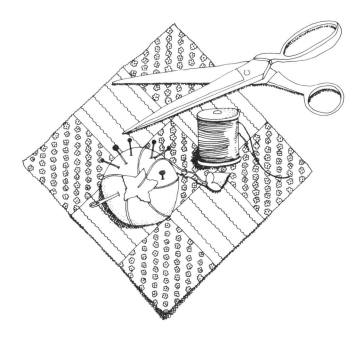

on poor-quality shears. They are more frustrating than we can even begin to describe. This is not a high-priority item for a beginner. For more on pinking shears, see page 109.

Rotary Cutter and Board

For confirmed patchworkers a rotary cutter and cutting board are a definite boon. They are expensive, however, and are not appropriate for a one-time quiltmaker. If you are (or become) a quiltaholic, a rotary cutter is an incredible revelation. You'll be amazed to see how it can cut through eight or ten layers of fabric quickly and accurately. Making a full-sized quilt with thousands of pieces can be a slow process, but after Betsy discovered the rotary cutter, she began whipping out one to two large quilt tops a week. This handy little tool helped turn a chore into a real joy.

Plastic Templates

Plastic templates in geometric shapes and strips in varying widths can be valuable tools and are worth the investment if you use them repeatedly. If you don't plan to use them a lot, skip the expense and make your own with cardboard or a ruler. By the way, a good plastic ruler will make a fine template if the size (width) is appropriate for your project.

Masking Tape

We use masking tape for several different things. When assembling a quilt and making the "sandwich," it's handy to tape the layers to the floor or work space. We've also used it to tape appliqué pieces to backgrounds to see what the overall work will look like or to enable us to move the pieces before they are pinned. Masking tape is optional, but it's very convenient to have around.

Patchwork

Patchwork quilts are probably almost as old as cloth itself. They've recently been photographed and documented in the United States dating back to the seventeenth and eighteenth centuries. When patchwork quilts were originally made by early American women, their purpose was strictly utilitarian—to provide warmth. Materials, often from cast-off clothing and household linens, were cut up and assembled into different configurations. Not only did the small pieces tell the quiltmaker's personal story, but very often the larger fabric patterns represented social movements and made statements about local history, current events, and religion.

Today most quilts have pattern names that evolved for them through the years: Log Cabin, with its red square in the middle to represent the hearth; Star of Bethlehem, with its religious significance; Double Wedding Ring, a traditional wedding gift; Whig Rose, with political implications; and patriotic quilts to support the American spirit. The list is endless, but don't be fooled by the generic-sounding labels. The quilts created by women generations ago are, in many cases, masterpieces. The colors and the designs are dramatic and innovative. The craftsmanship is phenomenal.

The dictionary defines patchwork as "something made up of an incongruous variety of pieces," and it's this jigsaw puzzle process that we enjoy so much. The old patchwork quilts with their many small pieces, magnificent color arrangements, and tiny quilting stitches are a constant source of amazement. It's mind-boggling to realize how much quiltmaking our grandmothers and great grandmothers did without the benefit of sewing machines or fabric shops where they could indulge in picking and choosing colors. Many of these one-of-a-kind creations hang in national museums and local historical societies where we can all see them and get our inspiration.

Although we do use leftovers and scraps from other projects, we also must admit to buying fabrics for specific quilts. This would have been unheard of 200 years ago. But it's a new era for quiltmaking, and we love the challenge of choosing colors and patterns and assembling the pieces into a well-designed finished product. It's also very satisfying to know that each quilt we make is unique. The pattern may be duplicated and some of the fabrics used again, but everybody's style and taste is different enough so that each quilt is personal and special.

The sections that follow will provide guidelines to help you get started with your own patchwork projects. We have listed the procedures that work best for us. But there are never any set rules, and as you gain experience, you'll discover what works for you.

One of the most exciting things about patchwork is how different configurations are grouped together. New patterns and designs are evolving every day. Once you get the knack of how pieces fit together, we hope you will experiment. It's a great challenge to make new and different designs.

PROCEDURE

Materials

assortment of cotton or cotton-blend
  fabrics
cardboard or plastic templates
pencil or ballpoint pen
scissors or rotary cutter (optional)
sewing machine or needle and
  thread
basic sewing supplies (see page 9)

General Patchwork Procedure

Step 1. Select the materials, wash them, and iron them flat.

Step 2. Select the design and make the templates.

Step 3. Trace the template shapes onto the wrong side of the fabric.

Step 4. Cut out the fabric pieces.

Step 5. Lay out the fabric pieces in the patchwork design.

Step 6. Sew the pieces together.

Step 7. Iron all the pieces flat.

Step 8. Sew more pieces together.

Step 9. Complete your patchwork by sewing and ironing, alternately.

Step 10. Finish your project, as described in Quilting (page 27) and Finishing Touches (page 40).

PREPARATION

Choosing Fabrics

Select colors and fabrics according to your tastes and needs, as described on page 4, in the amounts indicated before each project.

Clearing Away a Work Space

Choose a flat, hard, uncluttered spot, whether it be a table, bed, or area on the floor.

Assembling Materials

Gather all the materials you will need, such as thread, scissors, cardboard, and pen, as described in Supplies. The idea is to be organized so that you don't have to go running and hunting when you're in the middle of a project.

Making Templates

A template is a pattern for cutting fabric. Meant to be used over and over again, homemade templates are made of cardboard. Commercially made templates for repeated use are now available in craft stores and some yard goods stores.

To make a template, use posterboard or a lightweight cardboard box. Using a good ruler, carefully mark out

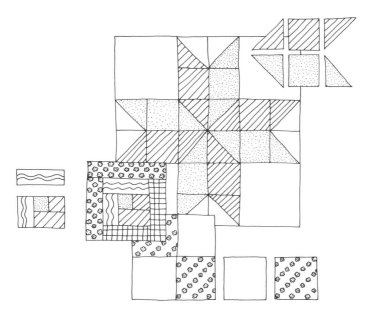

the shape you need according to the measurements given for each project. Cut out the shape carefully with scissors or a sharp metal-edged utility knife. Accuracy at this stage is very important. Slightly lopsided templates make incredibly lopsided patchwork pieces.

Make triangular templates by drawing a square first. Lay the ruler diagonally across the square being very careful to hit the corners exactly.

Templates and Seam Allowances

The measurements that we have given for each patchwork project and the templates for patchwork in this book include a ¼-inch seam allowance on all sides except where specifically noted. The foot of the sewing machine is usually ¼ inch. Use it as an auto-

matic guide as you sew. Don't forget that your finished patchwork will be correspondingly smaller when your stitching is complete.

GETTING TO WORK

Cutting Fabric

Lay out the fabric to be cut on a flat, hard surface, right side down. Using the template to guide you, trace out with your pen or pencil the required number of shapes for your project. If the fabric is dark, use a sharpened light-colored grease pencil or chalk. Although we advise beginners to cut one piece at a time for accuracy, more experienced needleworkers will want to save time by layering their fabric. They will be able to get through two to four layers with good scissors and careful cutting. Confirmed quiltmakers with a rotary cutter and a cutting board (described on page 12) will be able to cut through eight to ten layers. For most projects in this book, however, this would be definite overkill.

Laying Out the Fabric Pieces

With a diagram of your finished layout within view, place your fabric in the desired arrangement on a clear, flat surface such as a desk, the dining room table, or the floor. Lay out the pieces faceup as if you were assembling a jigsaw puzzle.

Clustering the Pieces into Strips: The Key to Successful Patchwork

Every patchwork design in this book contains a diagram for successful assembly, and we want to stress the importance of doing this step in an orderly fashion. If you break up your pieces correctly now, it will save a lot of aggravation later.

The overall idea is to assemble the patchwork into strips and then sew the strips together to form the whole design. But sometimes a design has so many pieces that you have to cluster and stitch them together first to create the strips themselves.

Every patchwork design is clustered differently. Sometimes, with the more complicated patterns, deciding on the most efficient arrangement for this clustering can take a bit of doing. If you study the Patchwork Receiving Blanket on page 53 and the Cat Shadow Pillow on page 71, you will see two examples of this process.

Pinning the Pieces

Once you have clustered the pieces into groups, you may want to pin them together in position for sewing to prevent the fabric from shifting. Many people prefer pinning all their work, while others find that they can successfully eliminate this procedure as they gain experience. It's all a matter of what makes you comfortable.

Sewing the Pieces Together

Remove two adjoining pieces from the layout and place them together face to face. Pin them together, if desired. Machine straight stitch along one edge to create a ¼-inch seam. Begin and end with a backstitch to secure your sewing.

Lining Up the Corners

This can be a touchy subject because different people have different ideas about perfection. Betsy once watched in horror as a friend tore out an entire section of a quilt because the corners were approximately ¼ inch off. It added at least two hours to her work time, but she would not have been satisfied with the finished results. We have found that if pieces are precisely cut in the beginning, they will usually fit together accurately. If they are slightly uneven in one place and you work carefully, the unevenness will correct itself later on. But more important, we feel that if the overall arrangement is successful, a slight imperfection will never be noticed. After all, to err is human.

Ironing the Pieces

For years Betsy made quilts thinking ironing was a waste of time. But the pieces puckered, and she ended up wasting even more time and losing patience trying to align them. Then, one Christmas she received a brand-new iron and decided to try it out on her patchwork. The results were astounding. Fabric pieces suddenly fit together quickly and neatly, seams lay flat, and the whole patchwork project took on a new, polished look. Betsy now has an ironing board set up in her workroom and thinks nothing of recommending that every patchworker follow suit. Jill, on the other hand, has her iron set up in the corner of her desk on an old towel. Mary Ellen Hopkins, patchworker extraordinaire, claims that it is possible to iron successfully on the arm of an over-stuffed chair. Do whatever works best for you, but if possible, we recommend having an iron available at all times during your project construction. For the most effective ironing, keep a spray bottle of water handy while you work.

After sewing pieces into increments or clusters, iron each facedown with the seams to one side. Do *not* press seams open. Spray liberally and iron smoothly but gently, being careful not to pull the stitching and distort the panel of patchwork. If it's appropriate, we suggest ironing the seam toward the darker side so it won't show through the lighter fabric. Iron at each stage of piecing along the way. Although it may seem unnecessary, trust us. In the long run, your projects will turn out better, smoother, and be easier to handle.

Quilt Assembly

Since there are so many ways to assemble a quilt, we have included an entire section on quilt construction. At this stage of your quilt, see page 28 for quilting hints and construction.

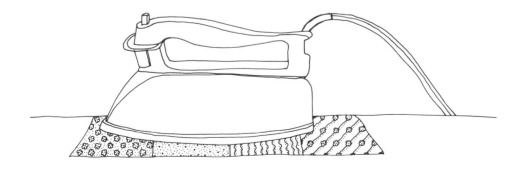

Appliqué

Appliqué is the technique of placing a small piece of fabric on top of a larger one and stitching it permanently in place. Whereas patchwork enables you to create magical geometric patterns, appliqué is the method to use for making lighthearted shapes such as cats, dogs, stars, and shoes. If you like to create pictures rather than patterns, appliqué is for you. And if you like to do both, even better. They look great when combined.

PROCEDURE

Materials

small pieces of cotton or
    cotton-blend fabrics, felt, ribbon,
    or other trimming as well as a
    larger piece of fabric for backing
cardboard for template(s)
pencil or ballpoint pen
tracing paper
carbon paper
scissors
sewing machine or needle and
    thread
embroidery hoop (optional)
basic sewing supplies (see page 9)

General Appliqué Procedure

Step 1. Select the materials, wash them, and iron them flat.

Step 2. Select the design and make the template(s).

Step 3. Trace the template shape right side up onto the right side of the fabric.

Step 4. Cut the fabric(s).

Step 5. Lay out the fabric on the backing material.

Step 6. Turn under the hem (if necessary) and pin or baste it into position.

Step 7. Sew the hem in place with hand or machine stitching.

Step 8. Finish your project, as described in Quilting (page 27) and Finishing Touches (page 40).

FABRICS FOR APPLIQUÉ

As we mentioned in our introduction, selecting fabrics is the most important part of any sewing project, and it's an exciting process to consider the options. For patchwork the choices are basically which cotton-blend prints or solids to use. For appliqué, there's a wider range of potential materials.

Cotton-blend Fabrics

Most of the fabulous appliqué quilts hanging in museums are made of printed-cotton fabric. Even today, cotton or cotton-blend fabric is still a great choice. Use it to create wonderful visual textures in colors and patterns that match your tastes and mood or decorating scheme.

Because it wears well and launders beautifully, we used cotton and cotton blends for the Scotty Quilt on page 103 and the bibs on page 98 and 100, as did Jill Obrig for her Cat Quilt on page 93. For more on cotton fabric, be sure to read the section beginning on page 4.

Felt

Felt, with its rich colors and thick texture, is also great for appliqué. Because of its ravel-proof edges, felt projects work up quickly and are incredibly satisfying to make. We used it for our I-Can-Do-It Book (page 109), Animal Hangers (page 125), and the Bears Shoe Bag (page 119).

Washing felt items can be a problem, however, and this has tempered our decision about when to use it. We have appliquéd simple felt shapes onto cotton tote bags, which, after months of use, we've tossed into the washer without much damage. But we wouldn't dare throw the I-Can-Do-It Book into the washer.

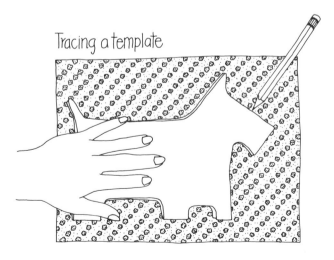

Tracing a template

Ribbon and Other Trimmings

Ribbon and other trimmings, such as rickrack and cording, are extra fun to appliqué because only the unbound ends need to be turned under and hemmed. But be careful to fasten all trimmings with strong stitches that cannot be removed by little fingers.

Most trimmings are machine washable, but check all labeling before combining it into any project.

DESIGNS FOR APPLIQUÉ— THE OPTIONS

All the appliqué projects in this book contain simple, medium-sized shapes, and that's because they are the easiest and most fun to do. In appliqué all edges have to be sewn firmly in place or else they will quickly unravel. Designs with a lot of intricate curves and crevices will drive you crazy if you are a beginner. On the other hand, skill with appliqué techniques develops quickly for many people, and you may soon find yourself eagerly tackling more elaborate appliqué stitchery.

You may choose to make our appliqué projects exactly as we have presented them, or you may decide to borrow images from one project to use in another. For example, why not use a bear from the Shoe Bag on bibs or cut 12 small cats from Jill Obrig's design and arrange them on squares in the style of the Scotty Quilt.

The possibilities for appliqué are endless. If you are partial to themes that we haven't included, such as owls or clowns, consider creating your own original shapes, either by drawing them or tracing them from a picture reference such as a book or magazine. Children's picture books are an excellent source for shapes to copy. Whatever choice you make, keep your shapes simple until you know what you can and cannot do with appliqué.

EMBROIDERY HOOPS FOR APPLIQUÉ

If you are using cotton or cotton-blend fabric and you decide to do your appliqué stitchery by hand, an embroidery hoop will keep your backing fabric taut, enabling you to make neat, even stitches. If you embroider on felt, however, you won't need a hoop because felt has so much body of its own.

Choose a hoop that's small enough to hold your backing fabric securely, but large enough to give you a substantial stitching surface. You'll be frustrated if you have to keep readjusting the fabric.

THREAD FOR APPLIQUÉ

If you prefer your hand stitches to be as invisible as possible, choose hand sewing thread or quilting thread and do tiny whip stitches or running stitches around your appliqué shape. If, however, you want your stitches to be a strong decorative element, choose embroidery floss or pearl cotton to do buttonhole stitches around your shapes. Crewel embroidery yarn is a good choice only for items that will rarely be washed, such as wall hangings.

For machine appliqué, cotton thread is best, though it's sometimes hard to find. Choose, in its absence, cotton/polyester blends in colors that enhance your design. And watch out! Machine appliqué is quick and easy and a lot of fun, but it really eats through thread.

For help in deciding on which stitchery technique to use, see page 24.

ENLARGING A PICTURE

To use any of the designs from this book or any other source, you will need to enlarge them to the appropriate size. There are several ways to do this.

Corresponding Grids

The most inexpensive and immediate method of enlarging a drawing is to use corresponding grids. To reduce a drawing, use the same technique in reverse.

Materials

tracing paper
graph paper (optional)
ruler
pencil
artwork to be copied

Procedure

Step 1. Trace the outline of the picture to be enlarged onto tracing paper or graph paper.

Step 2. With a ruler, draw a grid of equal-sized squares directly on top of your tracing. Number the boxes across the top and down the sides of the grid, as shown.

Step 3. On another piece of paper, draw a grid with larger squares. You may also mark out the bigger grid on graph paper using the ready-made lines as a guide. If you want your new drawing to be three times the size of the original, the new grid must contain boxes that are three times the size of those in the smaller grid. Number the boxes in the same way.

Step 4. Mark off with a dot in the same location on the larger grid each place where a line crosses the smaller grid. Keep the original picture nearby for additional reference.

Step 5. When all the locations are marked off, connect the dots to complete your enlargement.

Other Techniques for Enlarging and Reducing Artwork

Camera Lucidas, or overhead projectors, are perfect for changing the size of a picture. However, the inexpen-

Enlargement grids

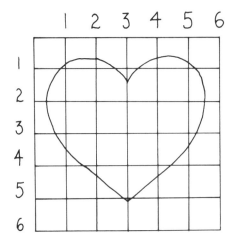

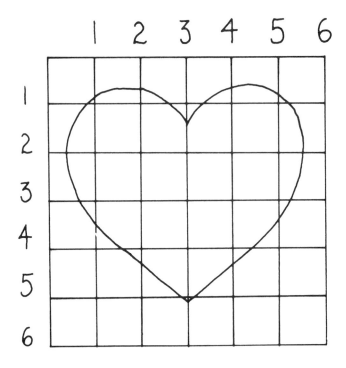

sive ones that are available in art supply stores have never seemed satisfactory to us. Schools often own high-quality Lucies, and if you have access to one, you'll find it a dream for getting the job done.

Although we have never used them, we have seen pantographs pictured in craft magazines that will enlarge or reduce a drawing as you trace the original. If you do a lot of appliqué, this may be a worthwhile investment. They cost less than ten dollars.

TRANSFERRING ARTWORK TO FABRIC

Once you have enlarged a design to the appropriate size for patchwork, appliqué, or embroidery, you will need to transfer it to the fabric. For the best results, be sure to iron all materials before you begin. Then, smoothing out any bulges, tape the fabric onto a hard surface. For patchwork, the fabric should be facedown. For appliqué and embroidery, it should be faceup.

We want to emphasize that it's very important to have a hard, flat desk or wood floor under your fabric or you won't be able to make a clear, visible transfer. This is one instance where a bed or carpeted floor just won't do.

Tape the artwork to be transferred face up on top of the fabric with the tape running along one side so it can act as a hinge. Place dressmaker's carbon paper in a color that will show up on the fabric you are using facedown between the artwork and the fabric.

Using a hard pencil or tracing wheel, carefully trace the design.

You can also use graphite paper for this, but we don't recommend standard carbon paper because it will leave smudges on the fabric. However, chalk or soft pencil will work well if you rub one of them across the lines to be transferred on the underside of the paper. Trace over the lines of the design firmly with a sharp point.

If you are using a light-colored fabric such as muslin, you can darken the lines of the artwork and then tape it to a sunny window. Tape the fabric over it, and trace the lines through.

Finally, if you are doing embroidery, you can pin a tracing paper or tissue paper outline of your design on the fabric to be embroidered. Stitch directly through the paper into the fabric. Pull your threads firmly so that they will sit flat when you remove the paper. Tear away the paper as you use it.

TEMPLATES

To complete any appliqué project, you will need to make a template or pattern to help you transfer the design to fabric. Templates are especially useful if you need to repeat your shape more than once.

Shirt cardboard is ideal for templates because it's easy to cut smoothly with sharp scissors and it retains clean edges after repeated tracings. Index cards, oak tag, and blotter paper also work well.

Making a Template

Step 1. Enlarge a piece of artwork from this book or any other source to the desired size, following the instructions on page 21.

Step 2. Using carbon paper, trace your design onto shirt cardboard or other stiff paper.

Step 3. Cut out the shape along the drawn lines.

Using a Template

Step 1. Wash and iron all fabrics.

Step 2. Place the template faceup on the right side of the fabric.

Step 3. Holding it securely with one hand, trace around the template with a pencil, chalk, or other bleedproof tool so that the outline is visible on the fabric.

CUTTING THE APPLIQUÉ SHAPE

If you are going to hand stitch your appliqué shape, or use a machine straight stitch, cut out your shape leaving an extra ¼-inch seam allowance on all sides. For easy hemming, use a scissors with sharp, long blades.

If you are going to machine zigzag your cotton-blend fabric in place or if you are using felt, you will not need to hem your fabric. Cut your appliqué shape directly on the traced line.

SEWING IN PLACE—THE OPTIONS

Let your temperament and skills guide you when you choose a stitchery technique for appliqué. Hand appliqué, Jill's favorite, can be a slow process, but it gives results with a traditional heirloom feeling. Machine straight stitching is faster, but you'll still need to sit patiently making hems.

Machine zigzag, Betsy's specialty, is for people who thrive on speed and efficiency. The results are more contemporary looking but extremely durable. Because it's so fast, machine zigzaggers find themselves sewing more quilts and worrying less about wear, tear, and stains on their creations—and there's a lot to be said for that.

HAND STITCHING AND MACHINE STRAIGHT STITCHING

You will have to hem cotton-blend fabrics that are to be hand stitched or machine straight stitched.

Hand Stitch and Machine Straight Stitch Procedures

Step 1. Cut out your appliqué shape as described in the previous section.

Step 2. If your appliqué shape is rounded, snip notches in the curves right up to the seam line for ease in rounding the edges. If your shapes are square, clip diagonally across the corners and neatly miter them.

Appliqué stitchery

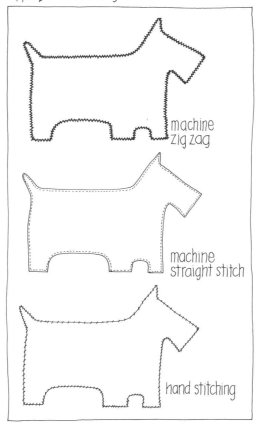

machine
zig zag

machine
straight stitch

hand stitching

Step 3. With the fabric right side up and the traced shape facing you, fold under the hem allowance with your thumb and forefinger.

Step 4. Baste all edges under. Use a large running stitch for easy removal later on. Or turn under the hem allowance and pin the shape directly in position on the backing fabric. You can also iron the hem under and then pin it on the backing fabric.

Step 5. Hand stitch the shape in place using a tiny running stitch or hem stitch. For a more decorative look, use the buttonhole stitch. See stitch guide.

Step 6. Remove all the pins and/or basting.

Step 7. For machine straight stitching, follow the procedure described above and do the sewing with a moderate-length stitch.

Machine Zigzag Stitch Procedures

Step 1. Cut out your appliqué shape, as described in the section on Templates (page 23).

Step 2. Pin the appliqué shape in position, right side up, on the backing fabric. Pins should be perpendicular to the edge of the appliqué shape so that the machine can sew over them.

Step 3. With the sewing machine set at 18 to 24 stitches per inch, satin stitch (zigzag) around the outside edge of the shape.

Step 4. Work carefully, checking to be sure that the edges are well covered by the stitches. Stitch completely around the appliqué shape and at the end, overlap your final stitches by about ½ inch to ensure that the stitches will not pull out. Machine-appliquéd shapes that are not properly stitched will pull away from the backing material. Shapes that *are* firmly attached wear like iron.

Step 5. Remove all the pins.

Quilting

The *Random House Dictionary* defines the verb "quilt" as "to stitch together (two pieces of cloth and a soft interlining), usually in an ornamental pattern." If a top and backing were just attached at the edges, it wouldn't be called a quilt, and there's a practical reason for this. Quilting holds the layers of fabric together and prevents them from shifting. Without it, the layers would slip, bunch up, and look awful the first time the quilt was used or washed.

In addition to this practical aspect, quilt stitching adds a special unifying element to patchwork and appliqué. Projects take on an extra dimension of importance and timelessness when they have been quilted. Once you see how quilting enhances your own work, you will understand why we include it, no matter how primitive our stitches. Although we admire the magnificent quilting being done by experts, we refuse to be intimidated. We are happy to quilt in our own style.

For first-time quilters, we have written the following overview. For specifics on how to complete your own quilt, keep reading.

PROCEDURE

Materials

patchwork or appliqué top or plain fabric

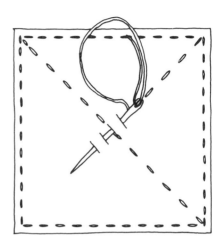

interlining or batting
fabric backing
masking tape
pins or basting thread
quilting thread and needle
bias tape (optional)
basic sewing supplies (see page 9)

General Quilting Procedure

Step 1. Complete the patchwork or appliqué top, or select a plain fabric.

Step 2. Assemble the backing, interlining, and quilt top. Prepare the layers for stitchery by pinning or basting them together.

Step 3. Bind the edges.

Step 4. Join the layers by some form of quilting—machine stitching, hand quilting, or tufting.

Helpful Hints for Quilting

*Wear a thimble or something protective on your pushing finger or you'll end up with punctured fingers. Betsy doesn't use a thimble, but she keeps a supply of Band-Aids with her sewing supplies and wears one each time she quilts. She's more comfortable when she can feel the fabric and finds a thimble very awkward. If you're accustomed to using one, by all means, do so.

*To lose the knot when you begin or end a thread, make a relatively small knot and pull it through the backing gently so that it gets trapped inside the quilt.

*With the present popularity of quilting, most fabric stores now carry special quilting thread. We recommend it. Heavier and slightly waxed, it is much stronger than ordinary thread. We suggest white quilting thread since it's fun to show off your handiwork.

*We have never found it necessary to use special quilting needles. Any relatively thin needle will do. Thick ones are hard to push through the fabric.

*When ending off, do so on the back side of the quilt. Pull the thread through a loop. Then to hide the loose end of thread, make an extra stitch into the fabric. Cut the thread close to the fabric.

*If your quilting (running stitch) pattern is intricate, lightly pencil in guidelines to follow on the fabric. The pencil marks will come out the first time the quilt is washed.

*When time is somewhat limited, you can combine hand quilting with either tufting or machine quilting. The red and blue Star Quilt, shown in the color photographs, is done with both hand quilting and tufting.

*When hand quilting, don't try to sew into the seam of the patchwork or appliqué. Not only will you be weakening the seam stitching, but you'll have a hard time trying to sew through so many layers of fabric. We suggest sewing parallel to the seams, about ¼ inch away.

Quilting Frame or Hoop

Betsy never uses a quilt frame or hoop because it seems to limit the portability of her projects. Jill likes to use the kind that sits in her lap. But plenty of quilters love their floor frames so we suggest you use whatever makes you the most comfortable.

The Filling

When you go to buy batting, you'll be faced with several decisions—thin versus thick batting, cotton versus polyester. Our overall recommendation is to use thin polyester batting. Although we'd like to be purists and use cotton, we've never had much luck with the results. Cotton batting pulls apart very easily and seems tough when you're trying to quilt through it. In addition, you will have to put in a tremendous number of quilt stitches to prevent it from bunching up the first time you wash it. Polyester batting maintains its puffiness better, is easier to sew through, and doesn't pull apart.

As far as thin versus thick, it's much easier to quilt and sew through thin batting. With thick batting, a quilt becomes very cumbersome, awkward, and difficult to stitch. Don't forget that in order for your quilting to be effective, you must stitch through all three layers of fabric.

Another option is to use flannel. Many years ago, flannel was frequently used as an interlining for quilts. It can still be used if you'd like, but it doesn't create as much texture as batting.

QUILT ASSEMBLY

When your quilt top is all sewn and/or pieced as described in the patchwork and appliqué sections, the two final steps are to attach the layers so they don't shift and finish off the edges with a hem or binding material. All quilters have their special methods for finishing a quilt, so naturally, we'll describe our favorites. They are the ones that worked best for us, and you'll see examples of them throughout *Welcome Baby*.

Quilt Composition

Placing the Layers. To assemble your pieces into a finished product, you'll need a flat surface slightly larger than the size of the quilt with enough room left for you to crawl around the edges, if possible. You'll be making a sandwich out of the backing, batting, and quilt top and it's worth taking your time at this stage to avoid a lot of uneven batting and frustration later on. A favorite shortcut of Betsy's is to tape

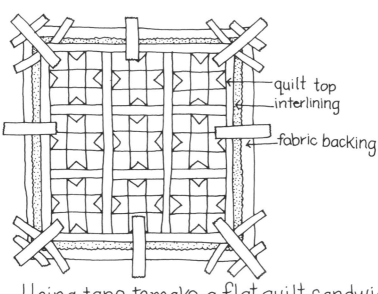

quilt top
interlining

fabric backing

Using tape to make a flat quilt sandwich

the corners down to the floor with masking tape as she lays out each layer. It keeps the layers from shifting.

The size of the quilt top will never be changed or cut after this point. Depending on the edging method you use, the sizes of the backing and batting can vary considerably. Their size, however, will always be dictated by the size of the quilt top.

To begin, lay out the backing fabric right side down on the surface you're using. On top of the backing, carefully lay out the batting, smoothing away all puckers, creases, or wrinkles. Place the quilt top on top of the pile with the right side faceup.

Attaching the Layers by Quilting

There are three basic ways to quilt: hand quilting, machine quilting, and tufting.

Hand Quilting

Hand quilting is our very favorite method, because we find it the most aesthetically satisfying to look at when it's done. For examples of hand quilting, see the Scotty Quilt, the green and pastel Star Quilts, and the log cabin pocket of the Baby Briefcase, all shown in the color section.

Hand quilting has several advantages. First, it really personalizes the finished product, adding great texture to the quilt that cannot be achieved by tufting or by machine quilting. In addition, if your quilt top and backing aren't in perfect alignment, it's simple to ease and distribute the fabric as you hand quilt to eliminate huge puckers or gathers. Another less obvious advantage to hand quilting is that it's portable, making it wonderful handiwork while visiting with friends or watching television. It also keeps hands out of the refrigerator. If you're working on a very small project, you may even be able to take it out while traveling on a bus or train. But be careful to keep everything on your lap, where it won't get dirty.

The disadvantage of hand quilting is that it's time consuming. In spite of that, we strongly recommend it. After all, you've spent a great deal of time, money, and thought on the project up to this point. Just plan ahead and allow a few extra days for those slow stitches. The results will be well worth the additional time. For this book, we deliberately kept the quilting designs simple, but the more intricate the quilting pattern, the more pleasing the effect, and we hope you'll try some decorative quilting designs.

Hand quilting is nothing more than a basic running stitch. Smaller stitches create more texture, are stronger, and will last longer although they're hard to perfect. But don't be intimidated. Do your best, even though your stitches may seem enormous, and you'll find yourself improving as you work.

Quilt one section or one line of stitches at a time, and depending on your quilt design, you'll be able to work out a direction for yourself in which to sew. Try to choose a direction in which you have as much continuity as possible and that will require the least amount of ending and restarting the thread.

METHOD 1. Thread your needle with a single strand of quilting thread about the length of your arm, and knot the end.

Bring the needle up from the underside of the quilt sandwich, through the layers of the quilt. Give a gentle tug to lodge the knot inside the quilt layers, or secure with a small backstitch.

Bring the needle down at right angles to the surface of the quilt, through the layers again and out the back.

Using this method, you will be able to control the size and placement of your stitches with ease, but it's slow going. Once you feel comfortable with the materials and tools, you will be ready to move into a more efficient technique.

METHOD 2. Begin as described for Method 1, bringing the needle to the top of the quilt from the underside and lodging the knot in the quilt's interior.

Then, take two or more stitches on the needle before pulling it through the fabric. Work along the top of the quilt and be sure you have caught all

Hand Quilting
method 1: one stitch at a time

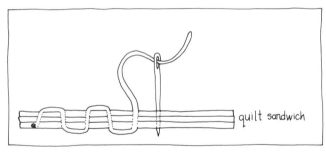

quilt sandwich

method 2: two or more stitches at a time

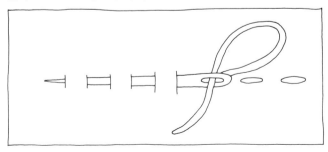

three layers of the sandwich on the needle before pulling it through.

It takes practice to perfect this technique, and the thinner the layers, the easier the stitching. If you are a beginner, choose the thinnest possible lining, as described in Filling on page 28.

Machine Quilting

This method will give texture to your quilt and can be accomplished much faster than hand quilting. It must be done slowly and carefully so that the fabric will be distributed evenly along the row of stitching.

To machine quilt, prepare the fabric as described above for hand quilting.

Put in pins perpendicular to the entire row before sewing. If it's not pinned, the fabrics tend to bunch up at the end of the row. Pull the fabric so that it's taut. Put in extra pins to prevent the quilt from buckling as you sew.

You can purchase a special foot for the machine called a walking or jump foot. It will help distribute the fabric evenly and will guide the needle so it "jumps" or "walks" over the thick seams. It also prevents the material from clumping up at the ends.

Use the longest straight stitch available on your sewing machine with natural color or unbleached thread. It's much stronger than colored thread and is available in most fabric stores.

For machine quilting only, always sew into the "ditch" or seam. The stitches will be buried or hidden and will create a wonderful puffy texture. At the end of each row of machine quilting, reverse the machine and overlap stitches for about ½ inch to reinforce the ends. Although many quilters swear that you must quilt from the middle of a quilt out to the edges, we have found that with machine quilting you can sew from side to side or at random spots in your quilt and be very successful.

Tufting

See the Patchwork Receiving Blanket and the red and blue Star Quilt in the color section for examples of tufting. This is by far the quickest way to keep

Tufting

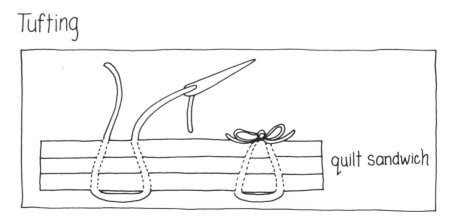

quilt sandwich

the layers of the quilt together and can be done when time is of the essence. Use cotton yarn or embroidery floss so that the quilt is washable.

Quilts can be tufted subtly in the corners of pieced fabrics or right in the center if you'd like an additional texture. We suggest that you use a very large-eyed needle to pull the yarn through the fabric layers. Tie it by hand. Again, the more tufting, the more efficiently the layers hold together.

To tuft, prepare the fabric as described for hand quilting. Make a stitch through all three layers with yarn. Make a knot on either the front or back of the quilt—the choice is yours. You may also consider tying a bow in the yarn. It is very attractive but optional.

Embroidery

Although the projects in *Welcome Baby* are primarily made with patchwork, appliqué, and quilting techniques, we have found that small touches of simple embroidery can add charm and importance to many items. If you are new at embroidery, we assure you that all of the stitches we use are easy to learn. If you are experienced, you already know how quick they are to do.

Please note that all instructions in the book are for right-handed people. Lefties who work in the opposite direction should be careful that the overall structure of their completed stitch is the same as what we have shown.

COUNTED CROSS-STITCH

One of the simplest of all embroidery stitches, counted cross-stitch has been used for centuries by people all over the world to decorate their clothing and accessories. The cross-stitches are all identical to each other, and they are worked into a fabric grid that keeps them evenly spaced and sized. But don't be fooled. Despite this rigid structure, the possible combinations of colors and patterns are infinite.

Fabric Backing

Although you can use practically any even-weave fabric for counted cross-stitch, we chose traditional Aida cloth for our Baby Sleeping Pillow (page 138) and our Welcome Baby Pincushion (page 141). It has 11 squares to the inch, which means that the stitchery works up very quickly and the results are terrific. It's available in a wide range of colors at needlework stores and in mail order catalogs.

Needle and Thread

For counted cross-stitch on Aida cloth, use #5 pearl cotton or two strands of embroidery floss with a long, blunt tapestry needle.

Embroidery Hoop

Because the cross-stitch projects in *Welcome Baby* are so small, we found that we didn't need an embroidery hoop. You may want to use one for larger projects.

Centering Counted Cross-Stitch

You'll be able to tell from our charts just how much fabric you'll need for your cross-stitching by counting the boxes in our graphed design and then counting off the same number of boxes on your Aida cloth. Be sure to leave 2 inches or more around all sides of the design for seam allowance. When planning the placement of your stitches, position the selvage edge on the left.

To ensure that your stitches fall where they are supposed to, we suggest you mark the outer boundaries of the design on the fabric with basting lines. Once they are in, count the threads again to determine the horizontal and vertical centerlines of the design area and mark these also with basting lines.

Beginning to Cross-Stitch

Begin to cross-stitch by putting in the stitches that are nearest the horizontal and vertical basting lines first because they will be the easiest to count accurately. Work back and forth across the chart, matching additional stitches on the fabric to those on the graph. Remove the basting lines by carefully cutting them away as they interfere with your stitching or when your cross-stitching is complete.

Secure the first thread by making a small knot at the end. Begin all subsequent threads by weaving them into the existing stitching on the underside of the needlework. End off with secure backstitches on the back.

Counted Cross-Stitch Procedure

Although all cross-stitches appear to be identical when properly made, there are several ways to do them.

METHOD 1. For the most even look, complete each stitch in its entirety before going on to the next. The first stroke runs from the lower right to the upper left, as shown. The second stroke, which crosses from lower left to upper right, should always lie on top.

METHOD 2. For quicker stitching, block in your stitches with half cross-stitches first, working them all in one

Putting in basting lines for cross stitching

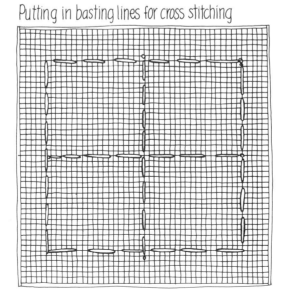

cross stitch: method one

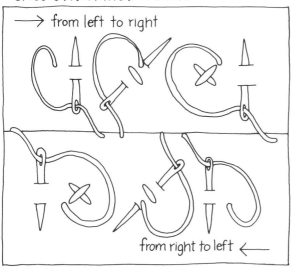

→ from left to right

from right to left ←

cross stitch: method two

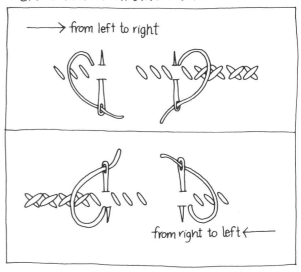

→ from left to right

from right to left ←

direction. Once you are sure that the stitches are where you want them, work back in the opposite direction to finish them off, as shown.

DECORATIVE EMBROIDERY

We used the simple embroidery stitches included in the next section to trim our Girl and Boy Rag Dolls (page 75), I-Can-Do-It Book (page 109), Bears Shoe Bag (page 119), and Washcloths (page 121). Because of the size and texture of the materials, we did not need an embroidery hoop.

Begin a new strand of yarn or thread with a small knot on the back of the stitchery. End off by making tiny, secure backstitches on the underside.

For all the embroidery stitching, we used a sharp embroidery needle and 6-strand embroidery floss, pearl cotton, or tapestry yarn. Specific size information is included in the Materials list for each project. We made our choices according to what stitches were in the appropriate proportion to the fabric we were using, and we hope you will adjust the size of your thread when you improvise projects of your own.

The Running Stitch

To make a running stitch for decorative embroidery, weave the needle in and out of the fabric keeping the length of the stitches and the space between them as even as possible. Work from right to left.

To make a running stitch for quilting, the procedure is the same except you'll find that your stitching is considerably slower. For effective quilt stitches, the needle and thread must catch all three layers of the quilt sandwich with each stitch.

The Backstitch

The backstitch is fast and easy. We used it to outline the letters on the cover of the I-Can-Do-It Book (page 109).

Work from right to left. Bring the needle up a short distance to the left of the beginning of the line you wish to cover. Bring it down to the right, inserting it at the beginning of the line. Bring it up again an equal distance forward along the line to the left. Continue working this way. Use the stitch chart as a guide.

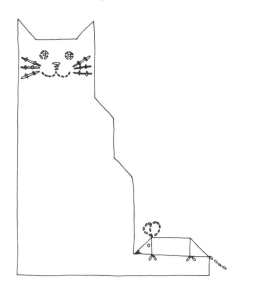

Stitch Guide

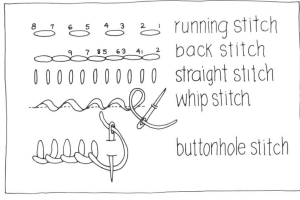

running stitch

back stitch

straight stitch

whip stitch

buttonhole stitch

The Straight Stitch

Make the straight stitch with the same in-and-out weaving technique as the running stitch. The main difference is that straight stitches are slightly longer on the surface than in the in-between spaces. Straight stitches are great for filling an area with texture.

The Whip Stitch

We have found the whip stitch to be an easy and satisfying way to hand sew appliqué shapes in place. Many people go on to cover their whip stitches with decorative embroidery such as the buttonhole stitch that follows, but we think it's attractive enough to stand on its own.

Use a needle and hand sewing thread to do the whip stitch. For strength, keep your stitches small. Work from right to left.

To begin the whip stitch, bring the needle up from the underside of the fabric about ⅛ inch in from the edge of the appliqué shape. Insert the needle slightly below and to the left of the edge of the appliqué and draw it underneath the seam allowance to the top of the shape so that the hem is held under, as shown. The thread will form a circle in a clockwise direction as you draw the needle through the fabric. When pulled firmly, the completed stitch looks like a small slanted line. Continue stitching around the appliqué shape until the entire edge is fastened. Bring the needle and thread to the back of the fabric and end off

with a tiny but secure backstitch or knot.

The Buttonhole Stitch

For the ultimate in hand-stitched appliqué, cover your whip- or running-stitched edges with buttonhole stitches. Use hand sewing thread to make small, whip-, or running stitches. Use embroidery floss or pearl cotton and a sharp embroidery needle to do your buttonhole stitches.

Work from left to right. You may want to draw parallel guidelines with a pencil to help you keep your stitches even. Begin by bringing the needle up through the back of the fabric at the left-hand end of the lower line. Then, holding the thread down with your left thumb, insert the needle through the upper line so that it comes out of the fabric on the lower line near where it first appeared. Make all subsequent stitches by pointing the needle in a downward angle so that the point comes through the fabric just below the appliqué shape.

The French Knot

A lot of people complain that French knots are too hard to do. Betsy is of the same opinion, but Jill is crazy about them. The instructions that follow are for her secret method to successful French knotting. Once you get the hang of it, she's sure you'll start making knots on everything. If her method doesn't work for you, we suggest you ask a friend, relative, or friendly needlework salesperson to show you how they make their knots.

The size of the knot will depend on the weight of the thread or yarn you use, so be sure to choose materials in a size appropriate to your project. Yarn knots would be overwhelming as eyes for the Carriage Dolls, but they would work beautifully as hair on the Rag Dolls. See Carriage Dolls and Rag Dolls in color insert section.

Jill's Foolproof Procedure for French Knots

Step 1. Knot the thread or yarn. Bring the needle to the surface of the material at the point where the French knot is to be.

Hold the thread securely between your left thumb and index finger close to the surface of the fabric.

Form a loop with the thread and bring the needle through it from the back. As you draw the needle through the loop, use the thumb of your left hand to guide the knot so that it forms directly on the surface of the fabric. If the knot is not sitting on the fabric, remove the thread and begin again. Once you get the knack of how to form the knot in the right place, you will rarely miss.

Step 2. Bring the needle to the back of the fabric right *next* to the knot, but *not* through it (or it will come undone).

If this is to be a single French knot, end off on the back with a knot. If there are to be others, bring the needle up again in the correct position for the next knot.

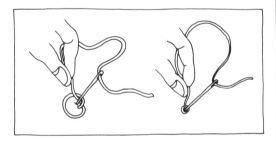

Finishing Touches

You may spend a lot of time piecing together a patchwork pattern or appliqué design, but until you finish off the edges of the fabric, your project is incomplete. There are many ways to finish a work, and we have included instructions for our favorite approaches. Read through these pages and choose the techniques that are most appealing and appropriate for you. We have found that spending a little extra time on the finishing touches can add tenfold to the visual impact and durability of a patchwork, appliqué, or quilted project.

FABRIC BORDERS

Attaching fabric borders is a quick, easy, and very effective way to increase the size of your quilt or pillow top. Many of the projects in *Welcome Baby*, from our patchwork crib quilts to the Baby Sleeping Pillow, are finished this way. In some projects we added double borders because we found that the "fabric frames" added grace and importance to our needlework.

We use the following technique to edge all sizes and types of needlework. After you follow our instructions once or twice, you'll discover how easy it is to prepare your borders by eye rather than worry about actual dimensions.

Materials

completed needlework top
fabric for borders in dimensions
given for each project
basic sewing supplies (see page 9)

Procedure

Step 1. Cut all the completed needlework (patchwork, appliqué, cross-stitch, or other) to the desired size, including a ¼-inch seam allowance on all sides.

Step 2. Cut four fabric borders to size according to the dimensions given for each project, including a ¼-inch seam allowance on all sides.

Step 3. Iron all the materials flat.

Step 4. Lay out the completed needlework panel faceup on a flat surface. Lay out the fabric borders faceup in position around outside edges, as shown.

Step 5. Attach the borders by placing the top strip face to face with the top edge of the main needlework panel, so that the edges are flush. Pin and machine stitch a seam ¼ inch in from the top edge. Repeat on the bottom edge.

Step 6. Remove the pins. Fold out the borders and iron them flat into an open position.

Step 7. Use the same technique to attach the side panels. Iron the borders into an open position.

Step 8. To add an additional border, cut fabric strips to size and repeat the above procedure.

Step 9. Finish the quilt top by binding the edges, as described in the section on finishing edges (page 42), or by turning it into a pillow according to the instructions on page 45.

PATCHWORK STRIP BORDER

After a quilt top is finished, you may want to enlarge it as we have just de-scribed to give it a framed appearance. You can construct the frame using plain strips of fabric or you can go one step further and create patchwork strip borders. Betsy used this technique to edge the Welcome Baby Pincushion (page 141) with tiny pastel-colored scraps of material. For the Scotty Quilt, she made a patchwork border by joining strips of the different plaids left over from the quilt itself.

The width of the border can vary according to your tastes and the size of your project, but we suggest that in many cases it should be between 1 and 2½ inches wide.

Constructing a Patchwork Strip Border

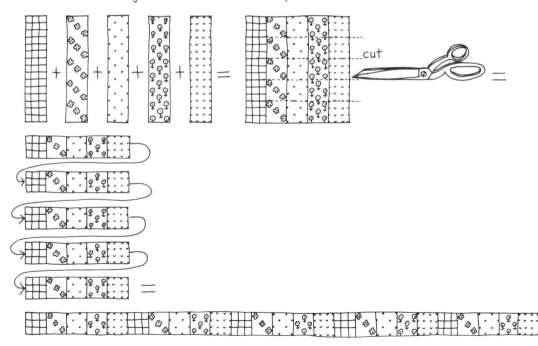

Materials

scraps of four to ten different fabrics
basic sewing supplies (see page 9)

Procedure

Step 1. Cut strips of each fabric approximately 30" × 2". Make one to three strips of each depending on how much yardage of each fabric is available and on where you are going to use the border. You will need a lot less for a small pillow than you will for a crib-sized quilt. See the diagram for the construction of patchwork strips.

Step 2. Sew the strips together lengthwise with a machine straight stitch leaving a ¼-inch seam.

Step 3. Cut the strips into 2-inch sections.

Step 4. Piece and sew the strips together so that you end up with one long strip.

Step 5. Cut the strips into segments of appropriate length to fit the sides of the quilt top or pillow.

Step 6. Attach the strips around the edge of the quilt top, pillow top, or panel to be framed with a machine straight stitch leaving a ¼-inch seam. See the preceding section on Fabric Borders for more detailed directions.

BINDING THE EDGES

When your quilt top is complete, you will want to bind the raw outside edges of the quilt. This comes at a time when the project looks messy—there are loose threads, uneven fabric, and bumps and lumps where there shouldn't be. But now is the time to clean up all of this.

There are many ways to do this job attractively, so feel free to experiment. In other words, don't feel bound to use the bias tape border on the Scotty Quilt just because we did. If you'd like the backing to show, try the fold-over method, or if you'd like a lace-edged border, use that one.

Bias Tape Edge

For a bias tape edging, all three layers (backing, batting, and quilt top) must be exactly the same size and should be cut to match up with the size of the quilt top when the layers are in place. (For examples of this finishing technique, see the Scotty Quilt and the Star Quilts in the color section.)

Lay out the backing right side down on a flat surface. Then lay out the batting and the quilt top faceup. Cut them all evenly. When layers are cut and the edges match up exactly, use straight pins to pin all around the edge. Place the pins so that they are perpendicular (not parallel) to the edge, about 4 to 5 inches apart. We also suggest you scatter a few well-placed large safety pins around the interior of the top surface. Be sure that they go through all three layers of fabric to keep the fabrics from shifting. Once the layers are securely pinned, the quilt can be picked up, moved, and sewn.

For baby quilts, we suggest using bias tape about 1½ inches wide. Some stores sell it by the yard and some specialty shops have printed bias tape, which can be fun to use for a slightly different or lighthearted effect. (The bias tape on the Scotty Quilt is pindot.) If you've used bias tape before and are familiar with it, use your own methods to put it on. If not, either follow the package directions or do as follows.

Lay out the bias tape on the quilt top along the edge. Place the bias tape so that it is right side down. Line up the edge of the bias tape with the quilt edge. Pinning bias tape seems unnecessary, but if you're more comfortable pinning it, please do so.

Sew along the folded seam in the bias tape, beginning in a corner about ¼ inch in from the edge of the tape and the quilt. Use a machine straight stitch for this. Go all the way around the quilt, easing and turning the corners gently. When you've gone all around, cut the bias tape and clip the

Binding the quilt edges

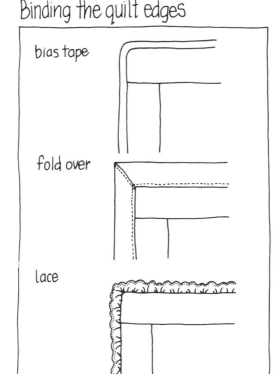

bias tape

fold over

lace

corners of the quilt carefully on a diagonal.

Flip and fold the bias tape over the back side of the quilt, tucking under the prefolded edge. Sew it down by hand using a hem or whip stitch. Finish the corner by folding under the raw edge and stitching. Remove the pins.

Fold-over Border

Betsy finds this to be the simplest and fastest type of edge to sew. For an example of this type of border, see the Receiving Blanket and Daniel's Quilt in the color section. You'll be making a sandwich of three layers of backing, batting, and quilt top again. However, the order is reversed when using this kind of border and backing.

First, lay out the batting on a flat surface. On top of the batting, lay out the quilt top faceup, leaving about 1½ to 2 inches of the batting showing around all the edges. (You can vary this according to your own preferences. If you want a very narrow border, leave less batting; for a wider one, leave more.)

Cut the batting to the border width desired. Do not remove the quilt top yet. Then, using safety or straight pins, pin the quilt top to the batting in enough places so that it can be picked up and moved. Set aside this section.

Next, lay the backing on a flat surface, wrong side up. To ensure that it doesn't shift, use masking tape and temporarily tape the corners of the backing to the floor or surface.

On top of the backing, place the pinned-together quilt top and batting faceup. Cut the backing, leaving a relatively wide border of backing (4 to 6 inches). At this point, remove the pins and re-pin the entire quilt, making sure to catch all three layers.

Next, fold over the backing to the front of the quilt. While you're bringing the backing to the front, fold about a ½-inch hem in the backing and pin it in place with the pins perpendicular to the edge. At the corners, fold one side of the backing first and then the other on a diagonal so that it will appear mitered.

Fold under the rough edges and pin them in place. When you've gone all the way around the quilt, sew by machine using either a zigzag or straight stitch. It can also be sewn by hand using a hem stitch. Stitch on the front of the quilt, about ⅛ inch in from the folded edge so that the hem is securely fastened. Remove the pins.

Lace Border

For an example of a lace edge, see the pink and blue Star Quilt on page 56. There are many ways to do a lace border around the edge of a quilt. We'll describe two equally attractive methods here.

"Inside-out" Method. Begin your quilt sandwich by first laying out the batting. The next layer should be the quilt top with the right side up. On top of the quilt top, place the lace with the

right side facing down and the raw (inside) edge of the lace aligned with the edges of the batting and quilt top. Pin the lace to the batting and quilt top with pins perpendicular to the edge.

The final layer is the quilt backing with the right side down. Pin it in place above the lace. (Do not remove the pins from the lace.) The edges of all four layers should be even and perfectly lined up.

Sew a seam almost all the way around the quilt about ¼ inch in from the edge with the batting side on the bottom. Leave an opening of about 8 to 10 inches. Sew slowly and carefully using a machine straight stitch. If you go too fast at this stage, the batting will catch and snag in your machine, so work with caution.

When you've gone around the edges, turn the quilt inside out through the opening and sew that part closed by hand using a whip or blind stitch. The quilt should lie flat. Sometimes it's too puffy or the edge doesn't seem sharp or flat, so if you're concerned about it, or if you'd like, you can make a row of machine stitching about ⅛ inch in from the edge of the quilt top. Remove the pins.

Fold-under Technique of Lace Edging. Cut your backing to exactly the same size as your quilt top. Then place it on the floor or surface with the right side down, smoothing out the fabric. Put the batting on top of it and cut it so that it is ½ inch narrower than the backing on all sides. Be careful not to clip the backing accidentally. Lay out

the quilt top faceup to align with the edges of the backing.

Starting in a corner, fold the ½ inch of quilt top under and toward the back, folding it over the batting. Pin the quilt top to the batting. Next, insert the lace between the quilt top and the backing. Pin the folded top (batting enclosed) to the lace. Do this all the way around the quilt.

Fold in the backing and re-pin the entire quilt with the backing attached. The top and the backing *must* be lined up evenly here or it will be difficult to sew. Sew all the way around the edges about ⅛ inch in from the edge of the quilt top. Remove the pins.

PILLOW CONSTRUCTION

Whether you make the Cat Shadow Pillow (page 71), the two-sided Carriage Dolls (page 84), or a Satin Heart (page 92), the final construction procedure is quick, easy, and fun.

Classic Knife-edged Pillow

Materials

pillow top
pillow back, cut to same size as top
straight pins
scissors
ruler or tape measure
pencil
sewing machine (optional)
hand sewing needle and thread
stuffing (polyester fiberfill available
   in yard goods shops and variety

stores) or pre-made pillow form made of fiberfill, kapok, or foam

basic sewing supplies (see page 9)
sewing machine (optional)

Procedure

Step 1. Select your pillow top. This may be a completed piece of needlework, a rag doll front, or an unadorned square of fabric. Determine the finished size and trim the top to the desired size, including the ¼-inch seam allowance on all sides.

Step 2. Select fabric for the pillow back and cut it to the same size, including the seam allowance.

Step 3. Pin the pillow top and back together face to face. Machine stitch around the entire top, including the

Knife Edge Pillow Construction

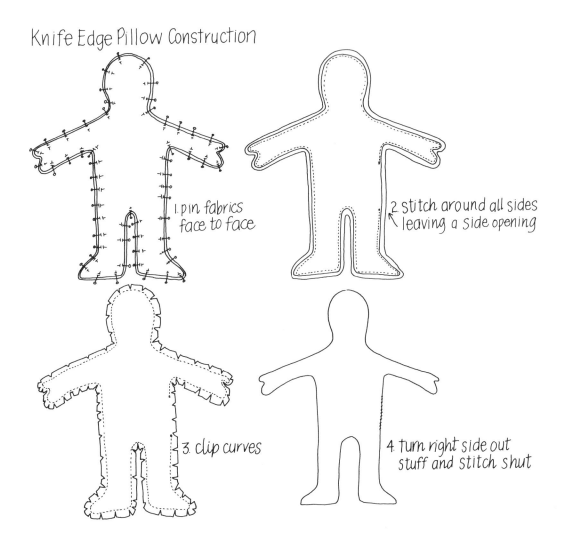

1. pin fabrics face to face

2. stitch around all sides leaving a side opening

3. clip curves

4. turn right side out stuff and stitch shut

four corners. Leave an opening large enough for reversing the pillow along the bottom. If the pillow shape is other than rectangular, machine stitch around the perimeter with an eye to leaving an opening on the side or bottom in a spot away from major stress.

Let the size of the pillow and the thickness of the material determine the size of the opening. Small pillows of lightweight fabric will need small openings while large pillows of bulky fabric will need larger ones.

Step 4. Clip the corners of a rectangular pillow and clip into curves of other shapes. Do *not* cut into the stitching. Turn the pillow right side out.

Step 5. Stuff the pillow with polyester fiberfill. Be sure to fill the corners with small amounts of fiberfill before adding the larger bulk. For small items, add the stuffing in tiny amounts at a time and push it into position with a blunt-ended instrument such as a crochet hook or surgical scissors.

Step 6. When you have stuffed the pillow to the desired density, pin the opening closed and hand stitch it shut with a whip stitch or hem stitch.

Box Pillow

For pillows with a three-dimensional look, consider the box pillow construction. Betsy made the patchwork Scotty Dog on page 106 with this technique. The *Welcome Baby* design on page 141 that we have made up as a pincushion would look great as a box pillow.

Box pillows are made with three basic pieces: the pillow top, the boxing strip, and the pillow back. The construction takes a little more time and patience than the traditional knife-edged pillow, but for that geometric effect, it can't be beat.

Materials

You will need the same materials that you used for the knife-edged pillow plus fabric to be used for the boxing (side inset) strip.

Procedure

Step 1. Select your pillow top, which may be a completed piece of patchwork, appliqué or other needlework, or a toy front such as our patchwork Scotty.

Step 2. Trim away the excess fabric leaving a ¼-inch seam allowance on all sides.

Step 3. Using a tape measure, determine the outside measurement of the shape that is to be your pillow top. This will be the length of your boxing strip. The width of the strip will depend on your personal preference.

You will have to hand stuff oddly shaped pillows, such as the Scotty, with fiberfill. However, for square or rectangular pillows you may want to consider using a form or other ready-made pillow lining. If so, the width of the boxing strip must conform to the thickness of the form.

Step 4. Draw the boxing strip on the wrong side of the fabric with a pencil and ruler according to the measurements you have chosen. Cut out the strip leaving a ¼-inch seam allowance on all sides.

For a patchwork strip, cut and assemble squares according to the instructions for the Patchwork Strip Border that begin on page 41.

Step 5. Pin one edge of the boxing strip face to face with the pillow front, easing the strip around the corners. Sew it in place along the drawn stitch line.

Step 6. Pin the pillow back face to face with the remaining half of the boxing strip, using the same technique.

Box Pillow Construction

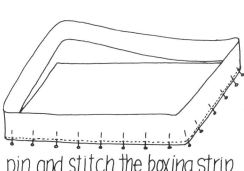

pin and stitch the boxing strip face to face with the pillow front.

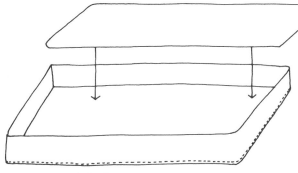

pin and stitch the pillow back to the remaining half of the boxing strip. Stitch, leaving an opening for reversing and stuffing the pillow.

Step 7. Stitch it in place, but be sure to leave a seam opening along the bottom edge large enough for reversing and stuffing the pillow. (If you are using a pillow form, the opening will need to be almost the same width as the form itself.)

Step 8. Clip the corners to ease the tension but avoid cutting into the stitching.

Step 9. Reverse the pillow, stuff, and hand stitch it closed.

The Projects

Even before our children were born, we found ourselves happily stitching quilts, bags, toys, and bibs for them. As they grew bigger, their need for diaper bags and carriage dolls disappeared. Betsy found herself graduating to bed-sized quilts (she is working on a monumental log cabin for her queen-sized bed as this book goes to press), while Jill refocused her stitching activities on making samplers and pillows.

But full-sized quilts and cross-stitched samplers take hours and hours to complete, and there was no way we could deny our love for making small, colorful, and fast projects for babies. As a result, every new member of our families or friends' families has been welcomed with a crib quilt, tote bag, carriage toy, sampler, or some other wonderful gift.

The projects that follow are a composite of items that we have made for our children and as gifts for other children. We have also included wonderful projects made by friends and a few things that we designed especially for *Welcome Baby*.

We've said it before, but we want to say it again just in case you skipped the introduction: Although we have provided step-by-step instructions for each project, please don't overlook the idea that *Welcome Baby* is also a book about choices.

Color, of course, is the first big area where you may want to make changes. Our quilt colors may not match your decorating schemes or tastes. Choose the colors that appeal to you. Our patterns will still work.

You may want to arrange your quilt squares in a different order. Though we have shown only a few, the possibilities are endless. You may also prefer to alter the proportions of the borders. Go ahead. As you work, you may decide to tuft where we have quilted or to use a star patch on the side of the Baby Briefcase (page 66) where we have used a log cabin design. Why not?

Even the size of a project is adaptable. Our Catch-all Basket technique (page 129) will work whether you use a 6- or 12-inch basket. Betsy has used similar baskets to give as gifts filled with fruit or other goodies.

Or, if you are feeling very adventurous, consider using the appliqué Scotty technique (page 103) to make another shape such as a cat, a house, or a truck. Stitch a child's name and birthday on the Welcome Baby Pincushion (page 141), or turn the pincushion top into a pillow instead.

But whether you go out and buy the same fabrics and colors that we used, or go off in your own direction completely, please have fun. We sew because we love the colors, textures, and patterns of fabric, and because we think patchwork, appliqué, and quilted items add a special enjoyment to life.

We stitch because we love it, and we hope you will too.

SAFETY FIRST

Although the projects in *Welcome Baby* are meant to be enjoyed by infants and young children, we advise you, as an adult, to use common sense at all times when it comes to safety.

Babies love to suck on whatever they can reach, so before you start make sure to wash all fabrics to remove the sizing that manufacturers add to keep their products crisp looking in the store. If you have chosen good-quality cotton-blend fabric with at least a 50-percent cotton content, washing will enhance the beauty of your project as colors and textures begin to soften gracefully. If, on the other hand, you have selected fabrics of pure polyester or of unknown fiber content, washing may save you from later heartbreak. If they emerge from the washer and dryer looking very much worse for the experience, you should reconsider your choice before you expend more time and energy on them.

Projects that are to be looked at by children but won't actually be handled, such as the Cloud Mobile (page 88) or the Baby Briefcase (page 66), need no prewashing. Unfortunately, we can't recommend washing felt items.

Other safety precautions we suggest include making frequent checks to be sure that all buttons, bows, and ribbons are firmly attached to their bases, securely fastening items like the carriage dolls to the carriage or crib, and seeing that toddlers use the I-Can-Do-It Book with adult supervision only.

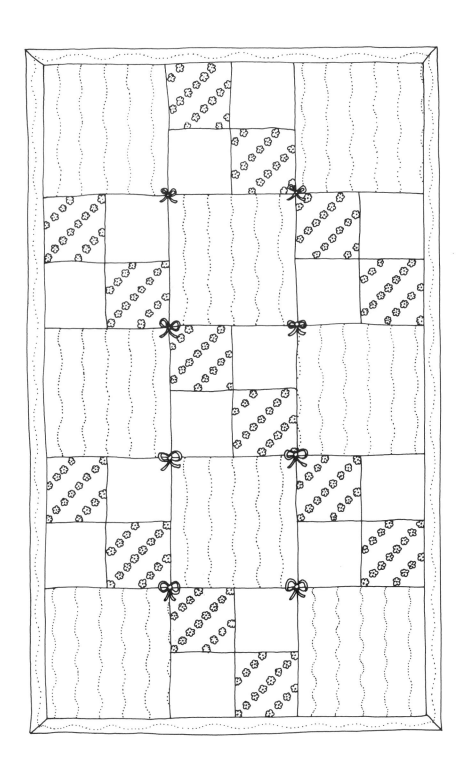

Patchwork Receiving Blanket

Because the receiving blanket is so easy to piece together and quilt, this is an excellent beginner's project to learn or to practice patchwork techniques. The flannel, which is inexpensive (we bought it in a dime store), is so-o-o soft that we wish we could include a swatch for you to feel. If this is your first patchwork project, be sure to read the Patchwork section that begins on page 13.

Finished Size: 24″ × 39″

Materials

2 yards printed flannel, part to be used as backing, part to be used for large squares on the front

¼ yard each of two other coordinating flannel fabrics, one solid, one printed

2 yards matching yarn for tufting
templates: 8″ square; 4¼″ square

Procedure

Step 1. Cut the backing piece to approximately 30″ × 45″. This will be trimmed down later. Using the templates, cut the following squares: eight 8-inch squares (same as the backing fabric); 28 squares 4¼″ × 4¼″, so that there are 14 each of the solid flannel and 14 each of the printed flannel.

Step 2. Lay out all the pieces in position, faceup on a flat surface. Begin to assemble the blanket by removing two adjoining small squares and sewing them together face to face with a machine straight stitch ¼ inch along one edge. Open the stitched squares flat and replace them in the layout.

Sew all the small flannel squares together in units of two. For this project, you will have to do it 14 times. When they are complete, iron them flat and replace them in the layout faceup.

Step 3. Stitch each pair to an adjoining pair in the layout using the same technique to form seven larger squares. Iron all the squares flat and replace them in the layout, faceup.

Step 4. Construct three rows, as shown in the diagram. Iron each row when the stitching is complete.

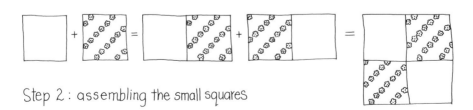

Step 2 : assembling the small squares

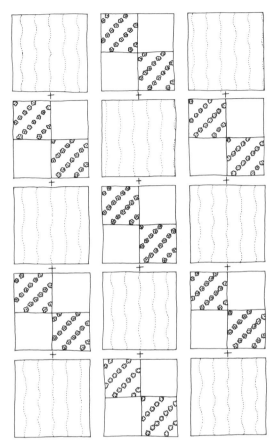

Step 4: constructing vertical rows

Step 5. Pin the three rows together lengthwise so that the seams of the squares line up. Sew the three rows together and remove the pins.

Step 6. Iron the completed patchwork piece.

Step 7. Lay out the backing on a large, flat surface, right side down. On top of it, lay the patchwork piece right side up. There should be approximately 2 inches on all four sides of the backing. Trim it if necessary.

Step 8. Fold over the backing to the front of the quilt. While bringing the backing forward, fold it under again with a ½-inch hem and pin it in place with the pins perpendicular to the edge. Top stitch all around the border using either machine zigzag or straight stitch. Remove the pins. For more on Finishing Touches, see page 40.

Step 9. With yarn in a large-eyed needle, tuft the entire receiving blanket in each inner corner, as shown in the illustration. Make a double knot first and then a bow so that the tufts will remain intact when the blanket is washed and dried.

Rainbow Bag

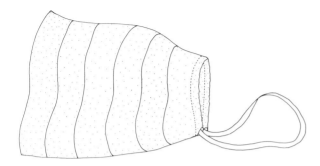

This is the perfect project for a beginner, and it is also one of the handiest items in this book. Use it for stashing toys, as a travel bag, or for storing baby's dirty laundry. Make this bag out of cheerful rainbow pindot, as Betsy did, or choose fabrics with a more muted look, according to your taste. Enjoy using the finished bag, and machine wash and dry it when necessary. If you're in a rush or want to coordinate the bag with another fabric, consider using one fabric instead of pieces.

Finished Size: 16″ × 19½″

Materials

¼ yard each of purple, blue, green, yellow, orange, and red pindot
1¼ yard ribbon or yarn for drawstring
basic sewing supplies (see page 9)
sewing machine

Procedure

Step 1. Cut five strips of fabric (purple, blue, green, yellow, and orange) to measure 34″ × 4″. Cut a red strip to measure 34″ × 5″.

Step 2. Lay out the strips horizontally in the order of the rainbow: red, orange, yellow, green, blue, purple. Stitch the strips together lengthwise one at a time, as described in the Patchwork section that begins on page 13.

Step 3. Press flat.

Step 4. Sew down a ¼-inch seam along both vertical edges.

Step 5. To make a channel for the drawstring, fold the top edge of the red fabric over itself, wrong sides facing, and press down a ⅛-inch seam. Fold again approximately 1 inch, press, and stitch along the bottom edge, being sure to leave the ends open.

Step 6. Fold the patchwork pieces horizontally, right sides together, and stitch across the bottom (purple) and up the side edge. Do not stitch into the channel for the drawstring.

Step 7. Clip the bottom corners on a diagonal.

Step 8. Reverse the bag. Insert a ribbon or yarn using a safety pin or bobby pin. Tie a knot in the ribbon.

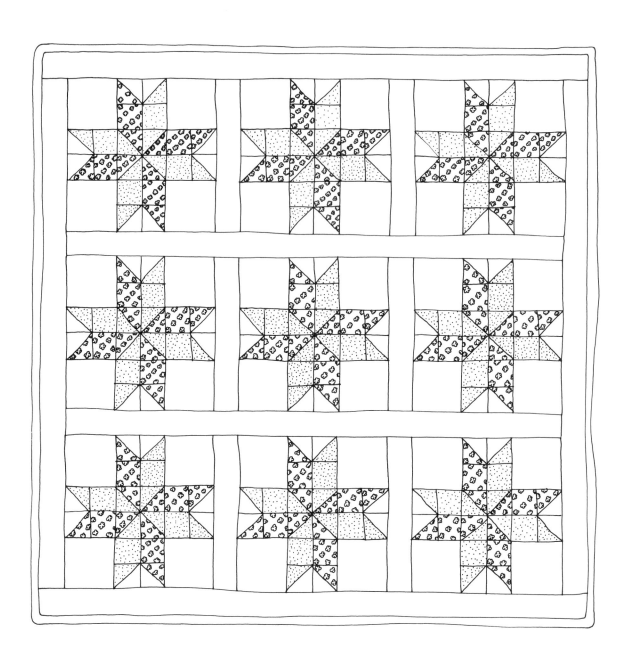

Star Quilts

When we talked about doing a book of baby projects, we knew it was important to stress how color choices can affect the overall look of a design, but we weren't sure how we could demonstrate it. Then a friend admired Betsy's first star quilt with the blue and pink pastel look, but said that for her baby she preferred bright primary colors. Another friend, also admiring the quilt, wondered how the same pattern would look in colors that coordinated with her living room where her baby would spend time on the floor.

Betsy stitched three quilts using the star pattern to encompass the color ideas of her friends. You will see them as you look through the color photographs. One is pastel pink and blue, one is primary red, white, and blue, and one is dark green and gray. We hope that you will use them as inspirations to assemble your own color combinations. For more on color options and ideas, be sure to read the section beginning on page 5.

Finished Size: 46″ × 46″

Materials

¼ yard each of nine different blue printed-cotton fabrics
¼ yard each of nine different pink printed-cotton fabrics
½ yard solid-color fabric (muslin)
½ yard blue cotton (solid)

1½ yards of fabric for backing (solid or printed)
quilt batting—48″ square
5 yards wide bias tape, single fold
templates: 3″ square; 5⅜″ square; 3½″ × 3½″ × 5″ triangle
basic sewing supplies (see page 9)
sewing machine

Procedure

Step 1. Using the 5⅜-inch square template, cut 36 squares of the solid-color fabric. We used white or muslin, but you may prefer another solid or a subdued print.

Step 2. Using the 3-inch square template, cut four squares of each blue print and four squares of each pink print.

Step 3. Using the triangular template, cut eight pieces of each blue print, eight pieces of each pink print, and 72 pieces of muslin or solid fabric.

Step 4. *A:* Lay out the pieces in the star pattern as shown on the chart. *B:* Stitch them together with a machine straight stitch, following the instructions on page 16. Be sure to follow the groupings on the chart.

Step 5. Press the completed star on the wrong side with a hot iron.

Step 6. Repeat this procedure to complete eight additional stars.

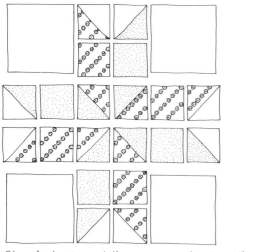

Step 4a: Laying out the pieces in the star pattern

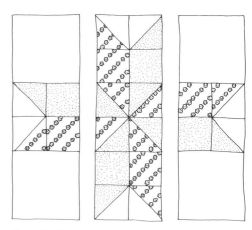

Step 4b: Assembling vertical strips

Step 7. Cut six strips of solid-blue cotton to measure 2″ × 15″.

Step 8. Attach the border strips to squares, as described on page 40.

Step 9. Cut six strips of solid-blue cotton to measure 2″ × 44″.

Step 10. Join the three rows of quilt sections, as shown in the diagram.

Step 11. Press flat with a hot iron.

Step 12. Lay out the backing fabric, right side down, on the floor or another large, flat, clean area. The backing fabric should be at least 4 inches larger than the quilt top on all sides. Lay out and smooth the batting on top of the backing. Lay out the quilt top, right side up on top of the pile or sandwich.

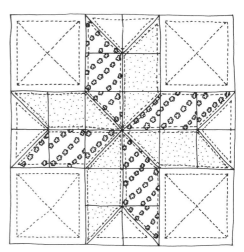

A completed star square with quilting

Step 13. Smooth out all the bulges and insert straight pins around the edge at approximately 4-inch intervals. Attach

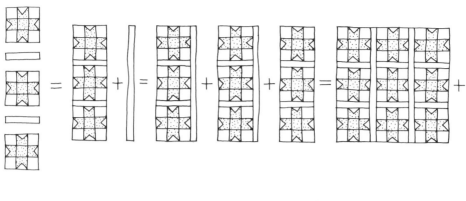

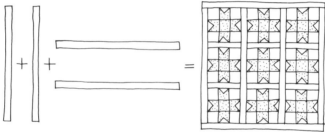

Assembling squares into a quilt top

four to six safety pins at random in the center of the quilt top to keep it smooth and prevent the layers from slipping.

Step 14. Trim the backing and batting to the same size as the quilt top.

Step 15. Attach bias tape around the outside edge of the quilt following the instructions on the package, or see the section in this book on Finishing Touches on page 40.

Step 16. Quilt by hand, following the quilt lines shown on the chart and using the instructions on page 30.

Patchwork Cat

Jill made a number of these cats from old quilt squares for the craft booth at her son's school fair. When she suggested to Jesse, then age 5, that he pick one for his own, he couldn't decide on just one so they kept three. These cats are easy to make with old or new fabric, and they make great gifts.

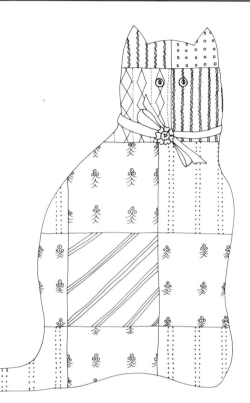

Finished Size: 7½″ × 10½″ plus a 6″ tail

Materials

9 squares of cotton fabric 2½″ × 2½″ (at least four different prints)

9 squares of cotton fabric 2″ × 2″ (at least four different prints; may be the same prints as in the above squares)

11″ × 14″ muslin

2 small buttons for the eyes (optional)

10½″ × ⅜″ satin ribbon (optional)

small silk flower (optional)

polyester fiberfill

basic sewing supplies (see page 9)

sewing machine

Procedure

Step 1. Enlarge the cat outline to the size shown, as described on page 21. Make a template, as described on page 14.

Step 2. Following the instructions for patchwork that begin on page 14, attach the nine 2½-inch squares to form a larger piece of fabric 3 squares × 3 squares.

Step 3. Attach six of the smaller squares together to make a piece of patchwork 3 squares × 2 squares.

Step 4. Sew the remaining 2-inch squares together in a row of three.

Step 5. Lay out all the pieces, as shown in the diagram, and attach them to make a larger patchwork piece.

Step 6. Center the cat template on the wrong side of the patchwork piece and trace the cat outline. Cut out the cat shape leaving a ¼-inch seam allowance on all sides.

Step 7. Place the cat shape face to face on the muslin and pin them securely. Machine stitch around all the edges leaving a 3-inch opening in the bottom for reversing the cat.

Step 8. Turn the pillow right side out. Stuff it with polyester fiberfill and hand stitch it shut.

Step 9. Sew on the button eyes securely. Tie a bow around the neck and insert a flower into the knot (optional).

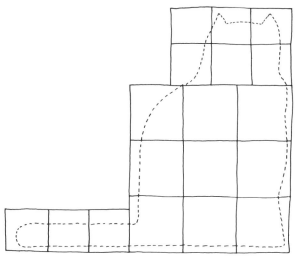

Centering the cat template on the patchwork

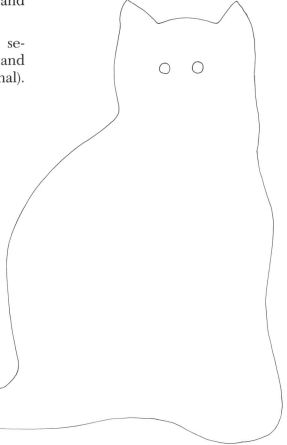

Baby Tote

Betsy designed her first tote for carrying Daniel's diapers. Daniel is now in junior high school with a backpack of his own, but Betsy still uses her faithful satchel for groceries, airplane travel, and trips to the beach. Because of its feather weight, she often tucks it away in a larger bag before setting out on an expedition just in case she discovers some irresistible treasure that she must take home. She's given similar totes in all different fabrics to her lucky friends, and it's fun to see the bags being used year after year.

Betsy's tote is strong yet it's ma-chine washable and dryable. We feel certain that you'll still be using it well after your baby is out of diapers.

Finished Size: 12″ × 16″ plus handles

Materials

⅝ yard quilted fabric
⅝ yard matching fabric for lining (solid, pindot, or subtle print)
3″ Velcro (optional)
basic sewing supplies (see page 9)
sewing machine

Procedure

Step 1. Cut the following pieces:

two pieces each of quilted fabric and lining fabric, 17″ × 13″

one piece each of quilted fabric and lining fabric, 41¾″ × 3½″

two pieces each of quilted fabric and lining fabric, 21″ × 3″

two pieces of lining fabric, 9″ × 7½″ (pocket)

Step 2. Construct the outside pocket by placing two pieces of 9″ × 7½″ lining fabric face to face and machine sewing a ¼-inch seam all around. Leave a 3-inch opening on the top for reversing the fabric, as shown in the diagram. Clip the corners on a diagonal, as shown. Turn the fabric right side out, making sure that the corners are pointed. Pin the rough edge of the fabric under and then pin it to the other side of the pocket and sew it together. Make a straight seam across the top open side.

Step 3. Center and pin the pocket onto the right side of one of the quilted 17″ × 13″ panels. The pocket should be about 3 inches from the bottom. Sew it along three sides leaving the top side open. Remove the pins.

Step 4. Construct one strap by placing a 21″ × 3″ piece of fabric face to face with the same size lining fabric. Sew on three sides, leaving the 3-inch end open. Clip the corners on the diagonal. Turn it right side out. Repeat this procedure to construct the second strap. When both straps are complete, use a sewing machine to put in a line of top stitching approximately ⅛ inch in from the edges around all sides of the straps.

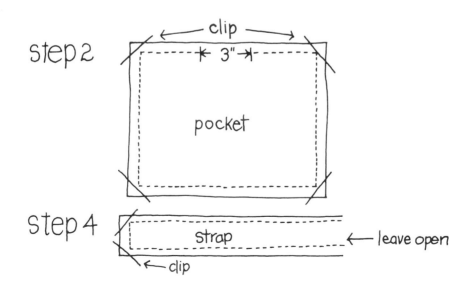

Step 5. Construct the inset panel using the same technique that you used for the pocket in Step 2. Because all edges of the inset panel will be visible when the tote is complete, fold in the open seam before doing the top stitching to make a clean hem on all sides.

Step 6. Construct the front and back panels next. Place the 17″ × 13″ pieces of quilted and lining fabric face to face. Sew with a ¼-inch seam as in

Step 4 for the straps. Place your stitching in from the sides, as shown in the diagram, and leave the middle of the top open for inserting the straps. Reverse. Push out the corners.

Turn in the raw edge and insert into the opening one of the straps that you made in Step 4. Pin the straps in position and sew a seam around the entire panel ⅛ inch in from the edge. Remove the pins. Repeat this procedure for the other panel.

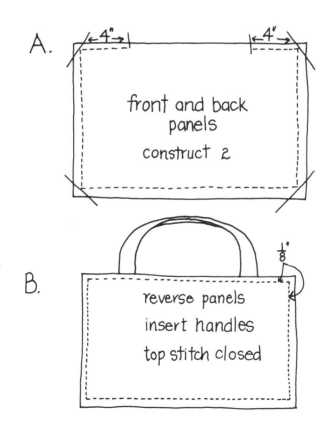

step 6

A.

|←4″→| |←4″→|

front and back
panels

construct 2

B.

reverse panels

insert handles

top stitch closed

⅛″

Step 7. Attach the side inset. With the linings facing and the large panel right side up on top as shown, pin and sew the side inset to the large panel with a ⅛-inch seam. Top stitch them together all the way around. Reinforce the seam by reversing the machine stitching as you begin and end your sewing. Flip over the bag and repeat this to complete the other panel.

Step 8 (optional). If you want a closable top for your tote, sew a 3-inch strip of Velcro about ½ inch from the inside top of the panel. Each half of the Velcro should be on the lining and centered between the handles. Machine stitch on the Velcro with a zigzag or straight stitch.

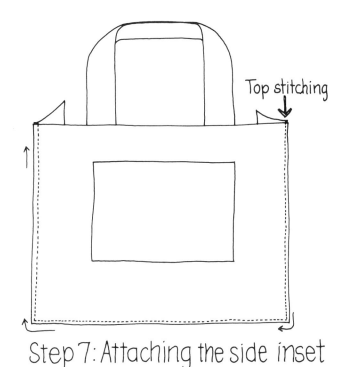

Top stitching

Step 7: Attaching the side inset

Baby Briefcase

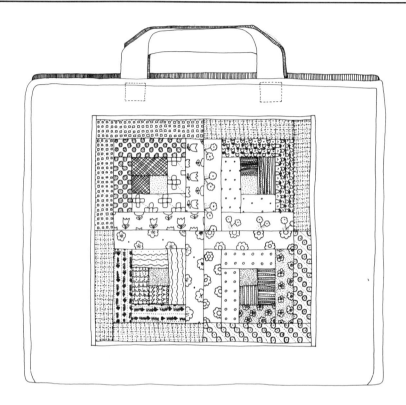

We designed the Baby Briefcase for those times when two hands just aren't enough. Because there are four roomy pockets, everything a baby needs is within easy reach. And when you pack to go traveling, you'll know at a glance whether you've remembered everything.

We put a log cabin pocket on the front of the briefcase because it's one of our favorite traditional patchwork designs. It's satisfying, full of surprises with the different prints and colors, and the individual squares work up quickly. But this spot is a great place to put just about anything, so you may find yourself inspired to choose another patchwork or appliqué design. Or, if you're in a hurry, use a plain piece of fabric for the pocket, as described on page 62 for the Baby Tote.

Finished Size: 13¼" × 16"

Materials for Basic Briefcase

16" × 26½" quilted cotton for the basic briefcase

16" × 26½" solid-color cotton for
the briefcase lining
quilted cotton for the inside pockets
in the following sizes: 11½" ×
8½", 11½" × 5", 11½" × 12½"
1 package of wide bias tape in a
matching color
15" × ½" Velcro in a matching
color
18" × ⅞" grosgrain ribbon for
handles
basic sewing supplies (see page 9)
sewing machine

Materials for the Log Cabin Pocket

⅛ yard each of four light-colored
printed-cotton fabrics
⅛ yard each of four dark-colored
printed-cotton fabrics
⅛ yard of solid fabric (preferably
red); the red square in the middle
of each square represents the
traditional hearth in the home
12" × 12" solid fabric for pocket
lining
12" × 1½" template
quilting thread and needle
basic sewing supplies (see page 9)
sewing machine

Finished Size of the Log Cabin
Pocket: 10" × 10"

Procedure for the Log Cabin Pocket

We hope that you enjoy the log cabin
pattern and may even be inspired to
stitch an entire log cabin quilt. The
technique is the same for a quilt as for
a small pocket piece, and the varia-
tions and arrangements of the squares
are limitless. If this idea appeals to you,
there are several good books available
specifically on log cabin quilts. See the
Bibliography on page 144.

Step 1. Using the template to guide
you, draw lines and cut two strips each
(44" × 1½") of the eight different
printed fabrics.

Step 2. Cut four squares 1½" ×
1½" each for the centers using the
solid (red) fabric.

Step 3. Begin with the solid square.
Place it face to face with a strip of
dark-colored printed fabric and machine stitch along the sides with a ¼-
inch seam. Trim the dark-colored fabric to the same length as the red
square.

Step 4. Using the same dark-colored
fabric, place the strip face to face with
the two joined squares and machine
stitch along the side with a ¼-inch
seam and trim the new strip to the
same length as the patched piece. See
the chart for further clarification.

Step 5. The next strips to be stitched
will be light-colored strips. Continue
working in an outward circular pattern, making sure that you always
progress in the same direction. Be certain to alternate using two strips of
light-colored fabric and then two
strips of dark-colored fabric.

Continue adding strips until there

Log Cabin construction

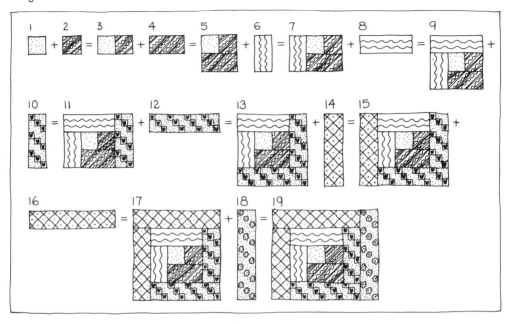

are four strips on every side of the red center square and until you have used four different light-colored prints and four different dark-colored prints.

Step 6. Iron the square flat and set it aside.

Step 7. Repeat the above procedure and make three additional squares so that you will have a total of four squares.

Step 8. Lay out the four squares in the desired arrangement. We have placed ours with the four light-colored corners in the middle. Machine stitch the

four squares together to form one unit of four squares.

Step 9. Cut four strips 12″ × 1½″ of the solid or red fabric. Sew two of them to the top and bottom of the log cabin panel with a machine straight stitch. Then stitch the remaining two to the sides. Iron them flat. See the section on Borders on page 40.

Step 10. Place the log cabin panel face to face with the pocket lining and machine stitch them together leaving a 4-inch opening for reversing.

Step 11. Reverse the pocket and whip stitch closed the opening. Iron the pocket flat.

Step 12. Quilt the pocket panel using a running stitch sewn lengthwise through the center of each strip. See the section on Quilting on page 27. Set the pocket aside.

Procedure for the Baby Briefcase

Step 1. Cut all the pieces to size, as described in the Materials list.

Step 2. Turn under and machine straight stitch the hems of all the inside quilted pocket pieces.

Step 3. Lay out the lining fabric faceup. Place the pockets faceup on the lining fabric. Use the illustration to

guide your placement. Pin them securely. Machine stitch the pockets to the lining around three sides leaving the top edge of each pocket open. If your machine can zigzag, do so. If not, use the straight stitch for the rest of the stitching in this project.

Pin and machine stitch a strip of Velcro along the vertical edges of the bag approximately ¼ inch from the top. When the stitching is complete, set the fabric aside.

Step 4. Lay out the quilted fabric that is to be the outside of the briefcase faceup. Place the completed patchwork pocket in position faceup. Machine or hand stitch the pocket in position.

Step 5. Place the lining (with the quilted pockets) back to back with the

quilted outside fabric (with the patch-work pocket). Smooth out all bulges and pin securely around the edges.

Mark the vertical center seam using a yard stick as a guide and machine straight stitch along this line. This will make it easier to fold the briefcase sharply in half.

Step 6. Bind all the edges with bias tape, as described on page 42.

Step 7. For the handles, center and pin a 9-inch length of grosgrain ribbon on each vertical side directly over the Velcro and seam binding. Be sure that the raw edges of the ribbon are tucked under. Machine stitch them in place by sewing a square, as shown in the illustration.

Step 8. To close the bag for use, fold it in half so that the Velcro strips will engage and hold the two halves of the briefcase together.

Cat Shadow Pillow

What's better than a cat on a pillow? Two cats on a pillow! We're both confirmed cat lovers, and we wanted to create a new and different feline design for patchwork. The resulting Cat Shadow Pillow is our favorite project in the book, and we think children will love it, too.

For the most striking effect when you make the Cat Shadow, choose fabrics for each cat that are in strong contrast to one another. Measure and cut your pieces carefully and be sure to assemble them according to our diagram. It's not difficult, but there are a lot of unusual shapes that must fit together like a jigsaw puzzle. For more on assembling patchwork, see page 16.

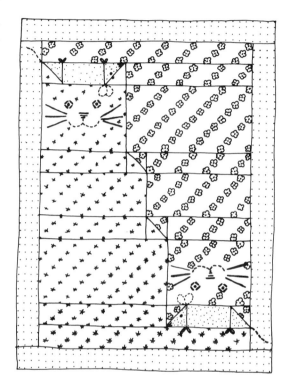

Finished Size: 12″ × 16″

Materials

¼ yard color #1 (one cat)
¼ yard color #2 (one cat)
⅛ yard (or scraps) color #3 (two mice)
½ yard color #4 (border and backing)
stuffing
6-strand embroidery floss—pink, yellow, white, green, and brown in tones that will be visible on the fabrics
embroidery needle
quilting thread and needle

basic sewing supplies (see page 9)
sewing machine

Procedure

Step 1. Cut the following pieces:

Triangles
two squares 2″ × 2″ each in colors #1, #2, and #3
Cut each square in half diagonally. You will end up with four triangles of each color.

Rectangles

one 10½" × 1½" each in colors #1 and #2

one 6½" × 1½" each in colors #1 and #2

one 6½" × 3½" each in colors #1 and #2

one 5½" × 1½" each in colors #1 and #2

one 5½" × 2½" each in colors #1 and #2

one 4½" × 1½" each in colors #1 and #2

one 4½" × 3½" each in colors #1 and #2

two 2½" × 1½" in color #3

two 14½" × 1½" in color #4

two 12½" × 1½" in color #4

one 13" × 17" in color #4

Step 2. Join the 12 triangles into six squares so that they are in the following combinations:

two squares of colors #1 and #2
two squares of colors #1 and #3
two squares of colors #2 and #3

Construct these squares by placing one color #1 triangle face to face with one color #2 triangle. Sew by machine straight stitch along the side of the triangle ¼ inch from the seam. Repeat for the other color combinations. Iron them flat.

Step 3. Following the diagram shown, lay out all the pieces, including the assembled triangles, on the floor or another flat surface in horizontal rows, as illustrated. Begin with the bottom row and work your way up. For the time

being, omit the border strips of color #4. Machine stitch into the horizontal rows by placing the pieces face to face and leaving a ¼-inch seam. Be careful to keep the width of the seams consistent.

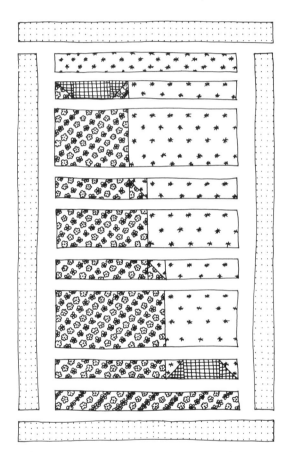

Step 3: Assembling horizontal rows

☆ color 1 ▦ color 3
▨ color 2 ⬚ color 4

Step 4. Iron each row flat.

Step 5. Lay out the horizontal rows and join them together by placing two rows face to face. At this stage you should pin the rows together to ensure that the corners will line up. Machine stitch with a ¼-inch seam. Work your way from the bottom to the top.

Step 6. Iron all the pieces flat.

Step 7. Join the border strips by first placing or pinning the side strips face to face with the cats, one on each side. Machine stitch with a ¼-inch seam. Iron them flat. Repeat this procedure to attach the top and bottom strips. Iron them flat.

Embroidery and quilting placement for the Cat Shadow

Step 8. Embroider on the mice and cat faces, as shown in the diagram.

Step 9. Quilt the cats, as shown in the diagram. There's only a little hand quilting here, but it adds so much to the look of the finished pillow.

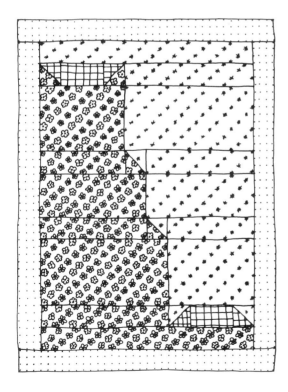

Step 5: Attaching the horizontal rows

Step 10. Pin the back of the pillow together with the finished front piece, right sides facing. Sew with the cat piece on top, facedown. Machine stitch all around the edge, but leave open a 4- to 5-inch space in the bottom to insert the stuffing.

Step 11. Remove the pins and reverse the pillow.

Step 12. Stuff, making sure to fill each corner as you go.

Step 13. Close up the seam with a hand hem or whip stitch.

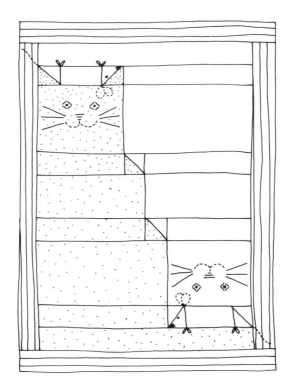

Girl and Boy Rag Dolls

It's so refreshing to see a child toting around a one-of-a-kind toy. We designed our girl and boy rag dolls with the idea that they might become somebody's favorite pals.

Both the girl and the boy are made from washable muslin, and the pattern is the same for each body. There are five simple body parts that fit together to give the dolls movable joints.

We want to assure novice sewers that the rag doll clothes are so simple that even a beginner will be able to stitch them by hand, although a sewing machine is a lot faster. The rag doll is a traditional homemade American toy, and because of its heritage, any improvising that you do will only enhance its personality.

We used linen dish towels for most of the clothing because we loved the plaids and we felt that toweling would stand up well to a lot of use. If plaids are not to your taste, however, flowered, gingham, or pindot cotton will also work beautifully.

Finished Size: approximately 14″ high

Materials for One Body

17″ × 10″ muslin
pencil
paper templates (see page 14)
polyester fiberfill
one 12″ strand brown yarn
one 12″ strand blue yarn
embroidery floss or pearl cotton—
   brown and red
tapestry needle
embroidery needle
basic sewing supplies (see page 9)
sewing machine (optional)

Procedure

Step 1. Enlarge the following body parts to the desired size, as described on page 21: head and torso (one piece), arm (one piece), and leg (one piece). Transfer to templates.

Step 2. Iron the muslin free of creases and fold it in half. Using templates as a guide, trace one head and torso, two arms and two legs. Pin the fabric securely to prevent slipping. Cut out all the pieces from doubled fabric. With a pencil, lightly draw on the features of the face. Stitch in all the features except the hair.

Step 3. Pin the torso and head piece face to face with the matching back pieces. Stitch them together ¼ inch in

from the edge of the fabric. Leave the bottom open.

Step 4. Pin the arm right sides together and stitch, leaving the end open. Repeat for the second arm.

Step 5. Pin the leg right sides together and stitch, leaving the end open. Repeat for the second leg.

Step 6. Clip into all the curves being careful not to cut through the stitching. Turn all the body parts right side out. Stuff them with fiberfill. Use surgical scissors or another blunt instrument to push small amounts of fiberfill into the tight areas.

Step 7. Place the legs side by side on a flat surface with the toes pointing up. Flatten together the front and back seam of each leg. Connect the legs with a line of basting ¼ inch from the open end of each leg.

   Pull on the basting thread to draw the legs together until they are small enough to fit into the opening at the bottom of the torso. Insert the legs into the opening and fold all the edges neatly under. Whip stitch closed the open seam.

Step 8. Fold in the seams at the end of each arm and whip stitch them closed. Stitch the arms to the sides of the body, thumbs pointing up.

Step 9. For hair, make French knots (page 39) into the head seam. For the boy keep the knots clustered at the top of the head. For the girl distribute the knots farther down the sides of the head.

Rag Doll Clothes (for both dolls)

Materials

two standard linen dish towels, approximately 18″ × 24″, in contrasting plaids

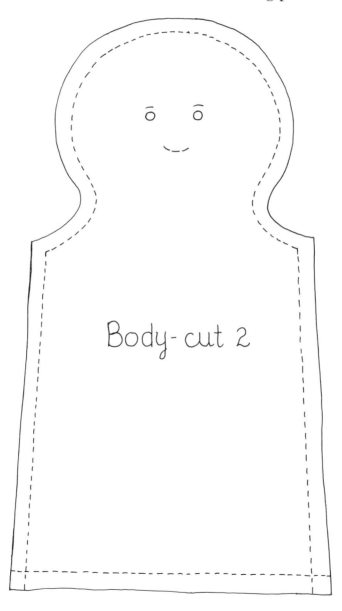

Body- cut 2

10″ × 12″ striped-cotton fabric
40″ ribbon ⅝″ wide
basic sewing supplies (see page 9)
sewing machine (optional)

The Pants

Step 1. Enlarge the pattern to the size given. Cut two pieces.

Step 2. Fold the top and bottom seam allowances of each piece to the back and straight stitch them to form hems.

Step 3. Pin the pants pieces right sides together and stitch down each leg ¼ inch from the edge. Stitch the inside seams, including the crotch.

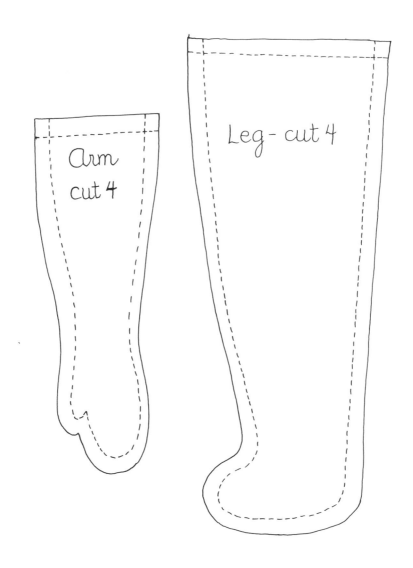

arm
cut 4

Leg- cut 4

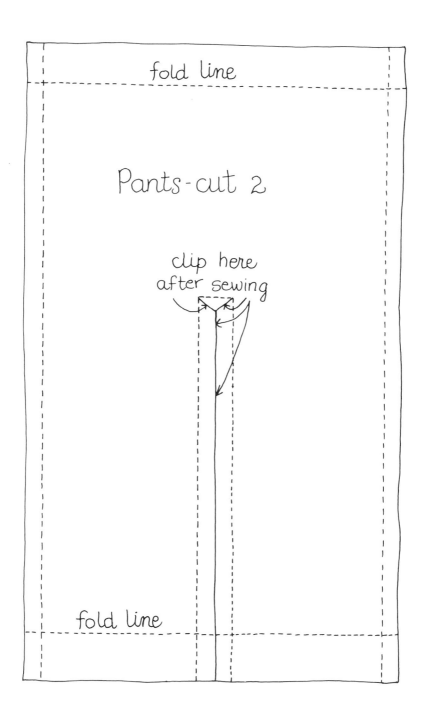

fold line

Pants-cut 2

clip here
after sewing

fold line

Step 4. Turn the pants right side out and slip onto the doll. Pleat the waistline on each side to the appropriate size and fasten it with a whip stitch.

The Shirt (Boy) and **Bodice** (Girl)

Step 1. Enlarge the pattern to the size given. Cut one piece.

Step 2. Cut the neckline by clipping the corners, as shown. Fold the neck hem to the inside. Press. Straight stitch ¼ inch all around the rectangle of the neck.

Step 3. Fold the sleeve hems to the inside. Stitch ¼ inch from the edge. Repeat along the bottom edge of the shirt.

Step 4. Fold the shirt in half horizontally, right sides together. Stitch across the arm of the sleeves and the down side of the shirt. Repeat on the other side.

Step 5. Clip the underarms. Turn the shirt right side out. Fit it on the doll.

Step 6. Gather a pleat on each shoulder and fasten with several whip stitches.

The Skirt

Step 1. Enlarge the pattern to the size given. Cut one piece. When doing this, line up the pattern so that the hem of the skirt is lined up with the finished hem of the dish towel. If you are using

fabric that is not hemmed, you will have to make your own hem.

Step 2. Cut and stitch the waistline, as described for the neckline of the shirt in the previous section, Step 2.

Step 3. Fold the skirt right sides together and stitch down each side. Turn right side out.

Step 4. Fit the skirt on the doll by gathering a pleat at each side of the waist and securing it with a few whip stitches. Fold in the excess fabric to shape the skirt.

The Apron

Step 1. Enlarge the pattern to the size given. Cut one piece.

Step 2. Stitch a ¼-inch hem on the sides and bottom of the apron.

Step 3. Gently gather the top edge of the apron. Center and pin 24-inch ribbon over the gathering.

Step 4. Top stitch the ribbon over the apron. Tie the finished apron around the doll's waist, over the skirt.

The Vest

Step 1. Enlarge the pattern to the size given. Cut two pieces of fabric in a pattern that will contrast with the pants. (We used blue-checkered and blue-striped fabrics.)

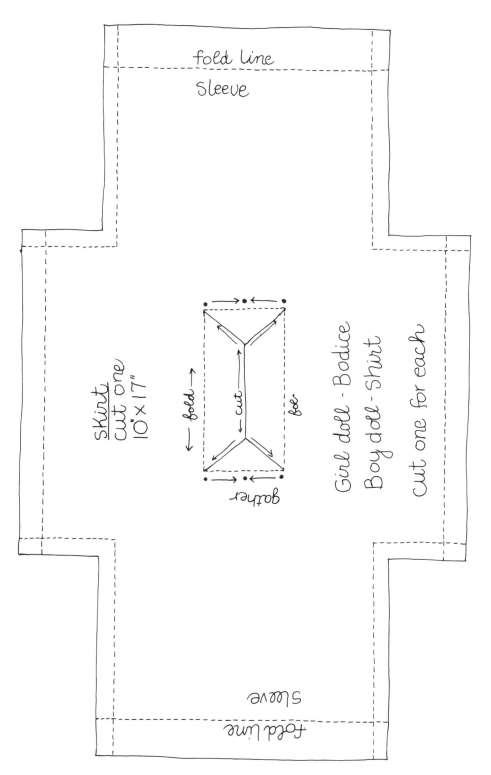

fold line

Sleeve

Skirt
cut one
10" x 17"

fold

cut

gather

bar

Girl doll - Bodice

Boy doll - Shirt

Cut one for each

Sleeve

fold line

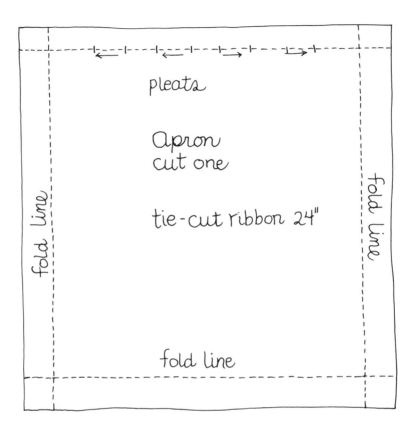

pleats

apron
cut one

tie-cut ribbon 24"

fold line

fold line

fold line

Step 2. Pin the pieces together face to face and stitch on all sides ⅛ inch from the edge. Leave a small opening on the bottom for reversing the vest.

Step 3. When the stitching is complete, turn the vest right side out. Turn in the open seam and hand stitch shut.

Step 4. Fold the vest into position horizontally and top stitch 1½ inches along each side to form side seams and armholes.

Step 5. Cut two 7-inch lengths of ribbon. Fold the ribbon faceup along the front edges of the vest. Pin and top stitch each piece in position. Fit the vest on the doll.

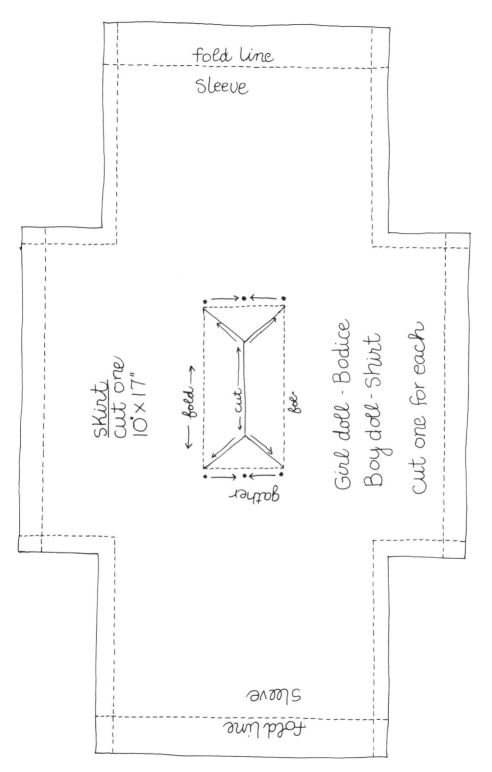

fold line

Sleeve

Skirt
cut one
10" × 17"

fold →

cut

← fold

box

gather

Girl doll - Bodice

Boy doll - Shirt

Cut one for each

Sleeve

fold line

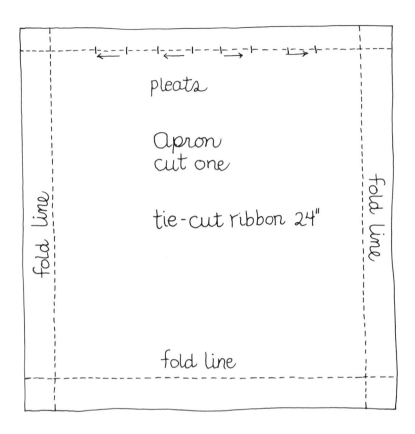

pleats

apron
cut one

tie-cut ribbon 24"

fold line

fold line

fold line

Step 2. Pin the pieces together face to face and stitch on all sides ⅛ inch from the edge. Leave a small opening on the bottom for reversing the vest.

Step 3. When the stitching is complete, turn the vest right side out. Turn in the open seam and hand stitch shut.

Step 4. Fold the vest into position horizontally and top stitch 1½ inches along each side to form side seams and armholes.

Step 5. Cut two 7-inch lengths of ribbon. Fold the ribbon faceup along the front edges of the vest. Pin and top stitch each piece in position. Fit the vest on the doll.

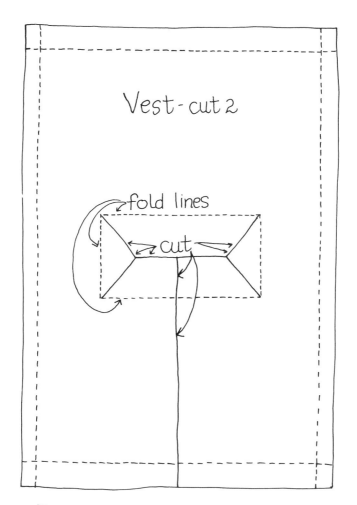

Vest - cut 2

fold lines

cut

Finishing the vest

top stitch the ribbon

↑ top stitch for arm holes

Carriage Dolls

Because babies spend so much time in their carriages and cribs, we wanted to make sure they would have some good-natured companions to keep them company, so we designed these little rag dolls. They, as well as the heart that accompanies them, are simple two-sided pillows that we cut into shapes, sewed, stuffed, and dressed. We chose to make our dolls from muslin and to dress them in muted colors, but they would look equally great with dark-fabric bodies or brightly colored clothes.

Finished Size: Each doll is approximately 5″ high. When they are strung together with the heart, the chain is 12½″ wide.

Materials

½ yard cotton muslin
¼ yard printed cotton
¼ yard solid-color cotton
fiberfill
embroidery thread—#5 pearl cotton or 3 strands of embroidery floss in the following colors: blue, red, brown
embroidery needle
60″ × ⅜″ wide ribbon
hand sewing thread and needle
basic sewing supplies (see page 9)
sewing machine

Procedure

One Doll Body

Step 1. Enlarge the doll outline to the

Patchwork Receiving Blanket
Catch-all Basket
Baby Sleeping Pillow

Apple Bib
Rainbow Bag

Star Quilt

Baby Briefcase
Girl Rag Doll

Baby Tote

Patchwork Cats

Carriage Dolls
Welcome Baby Pincushion

Star Quilt
Cat Shadow Pillow

Star Quilt
Baby Carrying Basket Pillow and Quilt
Boy Rag Doll

Cloud Mobile

Satin Heart
Rabbit Hanger
Cat Hanger

Cat Quilt

Daniel's Appliqué Quilt

I-Can-Do-It Book cover

I-Can-Do-It Book sneaker

Fish Washcloth
Bear Washcloth

Rainbow Star Bib

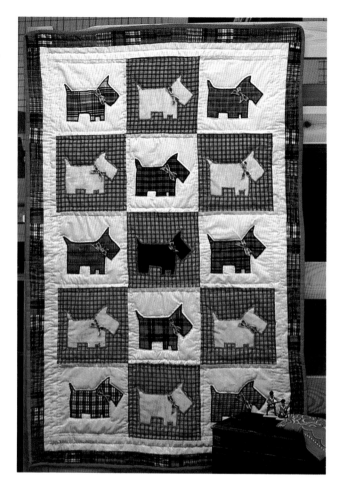

Scotty Plaid Quilt

Scotty Dog
Scotty Bib

Bears Shoe Bag

size given in the drawing, using the method described on page 21. Make the templates, as described on page 14.

Step 2. Iron all the materials. Trace the template onto the muslin twice. Cut out the doll shapes leaving a ¼-inch seam allowance on all sides. Trace the position for the eyes and mouth onto the muslin if desired. You may prefer to stitch on the face by eye after the doll is assembled.

Step 3. Place the front of the doll face to face with the back piece. Pin and machine stitch the pieces together around the outside edge. Leave a small opening in the side for reversing the doll. Clip the curves, being careful not to cut into the stitches.

Carriage Dolls

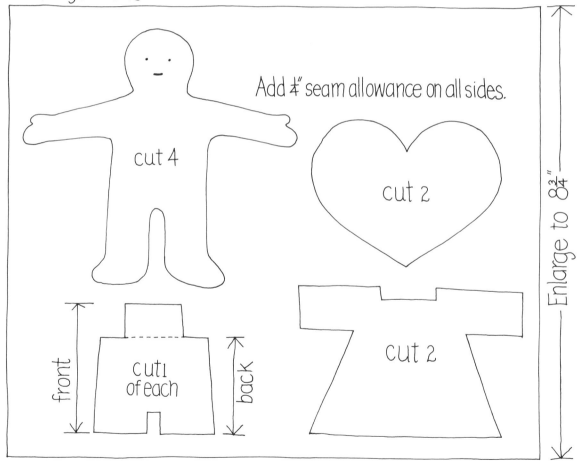

Add ¼" seam allowance on all sides.

cut 4

cut 2

cut 1 of each

front

back

cut 2

Enlarge to 8¾"

Step 4. Turn the doll right side out. Stuff it with polyester fiberfill. Push small amounts into the arms and legs using surgical scissors, a crochet hook, or another blunt instrument. When the stuffing is complete, turn in the open seam and whip stitch shut.

Step 5. Embroider the face and hair with French knots and straight stitches, as shown on the chart. Set it aside.

One Dress

Step 1. Enlarge the dress to the size shown in the drawing, as described on page 21. Transfer the enlargement to tracing paper and cut out the pattern.

Step 2. Iron all materials. Place the paper pattern on the wrong side of the fabric and trace twice. Or, double the fabric and trace the pattern once. Cut out the dress front and back with a ¼-inch seam allowance on all sides.

Step 3. Place the dress pieces face to face and machine stitch the shoulders, underarms, and side seams. Clip the curves, being careful not to cut into the stitching.

Step 4. Turn the dress right side out. Put it on the doll. Turn in the hem at the neckline, wrist, and bottom of the dress. Hand sew all the hems in place with a running stitch and doubled hand sewing thread. Pull the thread tightly at the neck and wrists to form gathers in the material. Put in a line of running stitches around the waist.

End off all threads with secure back-stitches. Set aside the completed doll.

Overalls

Step 1. Enlarge the overall front and back to the size given in the drawing, as described on page 21. Transfer the enlargements to tracing paper and cut out the patterns.

Step 2. Iron all materials. Place the paper patterns on the wrong side of the fabric and trace. Cut out the overall front and back leaving a ¼-inch seam allowance on all sides.

Step 3. Place the overall pieces face to face and stitch along the side seams. Turn the overalls right side out. Turn under and baste all the hems around the bib, the back of the overalls, and the bottom of the legs. Clip the corners where necessary to help make neat folds.

Step 4. Slip the overalls onto a completed muslin doll. Whip stitch around all the hem edges to attach the overalls to the doll. Put in the pocket outlines with a running stitch. Remove the basting.

Use blue embroidery thread or floss to make shoulder straps with a long straight stitch from each corner of the bib to the back. Set aside the completed doll.

Heart

Step 1. Enlarge the heart to the size shown in the drawing, as described on page 21. Transfer the enlargement to tracing paper and cut out the pattern.

Step 2. Iron all materials. Place the fabric face to face. Place the pattern on the wrong side. Trace the heart onto the fabric. Cut out the fabric leaving a ¼-inch seam allowance on all sides of the shape.

Step 3. Keeping the two heart pieces face to face, machine stitch along the drawn lines, leaving an opening on the side for reversing the heart. Clip the curves, being careful not to cut into the stitching.

Step 4. Turn the heart right side out. Stuff it with polyester fiberfill. Turn in the open seam and whip stitch it closed. Set it aside.

Carriage Doll Assembly

Once you have completed the two dolls and the heart, you will be ready to assemble them into a string for hanging in a crib or carriage or on the wall.

Step 1. Place the heart on a flat surface. Lay a doll on each side so that a hand overlaps the top of the heart, as seen in the illustration. Pin each hand to the heart. Attach the hands securely to the heart with whip stitches on both the front and back of the hands.

Step 2. Cut ribbons to size and fold them in half. Securely whip stitch each fold to the back of each free hand. Tie the completed string in the desired location.

Cloud Mobile

Since babies spend so much time on their backs, it's fun for them to have something cheery and bright to look at. Lani Hee made this rainbow mobile for her daughters, our children, and lots of others.

It's a great-looking project, but satin can be difficult to work on because it frays easily when handled. If you're a novice but are interested in this mobile, we suggest doing it with brightly colored solid cotton or felt, using the same pattern.

Finished Size: cloud and ribbons—
approximately 6″ × 9″
star—approximately 5″ × 5″
overall length when hanging—24″ or
more

Materials

7″ satin ribbon in each of the
following colors: red, purple, blue,
green, yellow, orange
¼ yard (or scraps) white satin,
cotton, or felt (for the cloud)
¼ yard (or scraps) yellow satin,
cotton, or felt (for the star)
quilting thread, yarn, string, or
fishing line to hang the mobile
basic sewing supplies (see page 9)

Procedure

Step 1. Trace artwork as shown. Cut the cloud pieces, star pieces, and ribbons. *Caution:* Remember that you can't handle satin too much because it frays easily.

Step 2. Place the cloud pieces together face to face and sew across the top.

Step 3. Reverse the cloud.

Step 4. Turn under the seam allowance of the cloud and iron it flat.

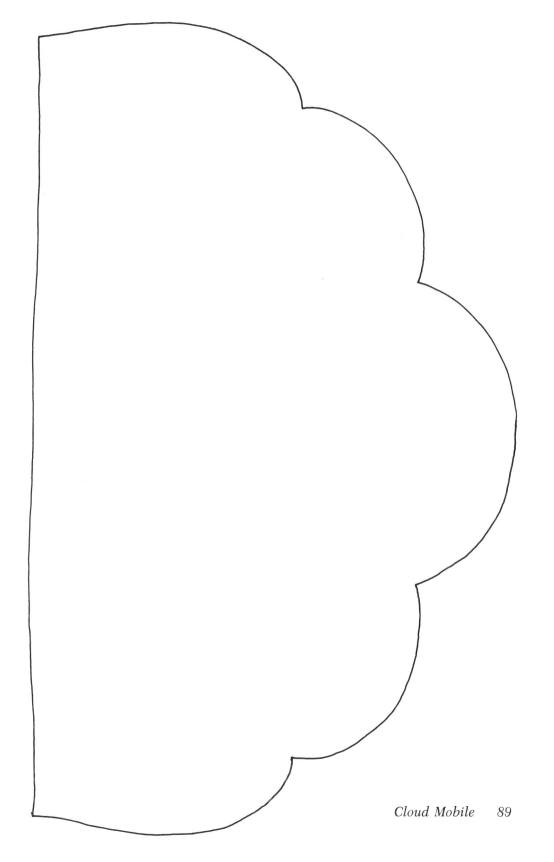

Step 5. Insert the ribbon into the seam at the bottom edges and pin it so it is against the hem of the seam allowance on one side.

Step 6. Machine stitch onto the folded seam using a long straight stitch to attach the ribbons, but do not stitch the cloud shut.

Step 7. Fill the cloud with stuffing.

Step 8. Pin the seam allowances together and hand stitch them closed, using the hem stitch or whip stitch.

Step 9. Trim the ribbons on the bottom with a diagonal edge.

Step 10. Cut two star pieces. Place them face to face. Machine stitch the star leaving one edge open.

Step 11. Reverse the star. Work slowly because satin is incredibly perishable. Push out the tips of the star very carefully by inserting a pin in the seams and working toward each point.

Step 12. Stuff the star carefully using surgical scissors or blunt tweezers to insert the stuffing.

Step 13. Hand stitch the star closed, using a whip or hem stitch.

Step 14. Insert quilting thread through the top of the star. Tie a knot under the star so that the star can't slip down. Insert the quilting thread through the top of the cloud and out the bottom. Make another knot to hold the cloud in place. Hang the completed mobile with a Christmas tree hook from the ceiling or window.

Satin Heart

While we were photographing the projects for *Welcome Baby* in the bedroom of six-year-old Alicia Colen, we discovered a wonderful pink satin heart on her bed. We couldn't resist including it in our book, and you'll see it a few times in the color photographs. Although Alicia received it as a gift and the maker is unknown, you can easily make your own satin heart if you enlarge the heart outline that we have given for the Carriage Dolls on page 84. Be sure to read the comments on sewing with satin that we have included with the Cloud Mobile (page 88). If you are especially eager to make a satin accessory (they are so appealing!), this might be a good first project. For your babies, we suggest hanging the heart in a window or on the wall as a mobile. You might also consider using bright-red satin for a more eye-catching effect.

Finished Size: approximately 8″ × 8″

Materials

2 pieces of satin 9″ × 9″ each
polyester fiberfill
quilting thread or fishing line to hang the heart (optional)
basic sewing supplies (see page 9)
sewing machine (optional)

Procedure

Step 1. Enlarge the heart outline to 8 inches, according to the instructions on page 21.

Step 2. Cut out the heart shape and trace it onto the back of the satin pieces. Cut out the fabric hearts leaving a ¼-inch seam allowance on all sides.

Step 3. Sew the hearts together face to face. Leave a 2-inch opening along one side for reversing the heart. Begin and end the sewing with a backstitch. Clip into the curves of the heart, being careful not to cut through the stitching.

Step 4. Turn the heart right side out. Stuff it with fiberfill until you reach the desired density. Turn in the open seam and hand stitch it closed.

Step 5. If you plan to hang the heart, cut the quilting thread or fishing line to the desired length. Attach it to the heart with a few whip stitches. Hang the finished heart in a window or on a wall.

Cat Quilt

Jill Obrig made this wonderful cat quilt while she was pregnant. As you can see from Jill's photograph in the color section, Michelle, 8 months old at this writing, just loves it.

For her cat shape, Jill traced the outline of a cat and ball from a photograph and enlarged it to the right size for her baby quilt. She cut the cat and ball from one piece of fabric and appliquéd them to the backing with a machine zigzag stitch.

To add dimension to her cat and ball, Jill carefully made two incisions on the underside of the quilt and gently stuffed the shapes with polyester fiberfill. She completed the quilt with tufting.

Finished Size: 34″ × 42″

Materials

18″ × 25″ printed fabric in a dark color for the cat and the ball

30″ × 38″ (plus seam allowance) printed fabric in a light color for the appliqué backing

fabric strips for the border in the same print as the cat in the following dimensions:

two strips 30″ × 2″ plus seam allowance

two strips 40″ × 2″ plus seam allowance

34″ × 42″ cotton fabric for the quilt back

polyester fiberfill to stuff the cat and the ball

embroidery floss or yarn for tufting

basic sewing supplies (see page 9)

sewing machine

Procedure

Step 1. Enlarge the cat and ball to approximately 25″ × 18″, according to the instructions on page 21.

Trace the cat and ball shape onto the right side of the fabric and cut out the shape on the drawn line for machine zigzag appliqué. If you are going to appliqué by hand, see the instructions that begin on page 24.

Step 2. Pin the cat and ball in place, faceup on the right side of the fabric backing. Machine zigzag them in place so that the edge of the appliqué shape is held firmly in place by the stitching.

Step 3. When the stitching is complete, remove the pins and turn the quilt over. With a pointed scissors, carefully make a 3-inch incision in the backing in the middle of the cat outline. *Be careful not to cut into the cat appliqué itself.* Fill the cat shape with small amounts of polyester fiberfill. When you reach the desired density, stitch up the incision by hand. Repeat this procedure to fill the ball, making a shorter incision.

Step 4. Add the fabric borders, as described on page 40.

Step 5. Place the quilt top face to face with the backing fabric. Pin them together and machine stitch around the outside edges, leaving a 5-inch opening along one side for reversing the quilt.

Turn the quilt right side out. Turn in the open seam and hand stitch it closed.

Step 6. Secure the front and back layers of the quilt by smoothing them out and tying little knots using the embroidery floss or yarn. The knots should be about 5 inches apart. Do not place the knots (or tufting) within the cat shape.

For alternate ways of finishing this quilt, turn to page 30.

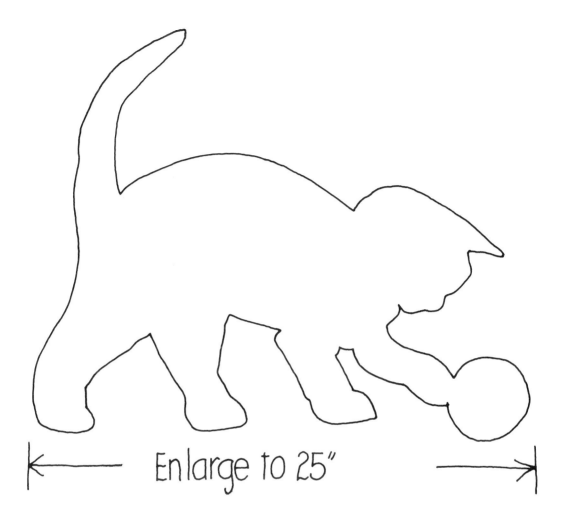

Enlarge to 25″

Daniel's Appliqué Quilt

When Jesse Jarnow was born, Betsy's six-year-old son, Daniel, made his new cousin a baby quilt. It hangs on the wall above Jesse's bed and Jesse, now six himself, loves looking at it and knowing that his older cousin Daniel made it for him when he was just the same age.

Of course, Betsy did the sewing on this project, but the designing, cutting, and supervising was done by Daniel, who was allowed to rummage through Betsy's fabric collection and choose colors and patterns that he liked. He cut them into shapes and sat with his mother while she machine appliquéd them to the backing fabric.

If you have a child who is old enough to cut fabric, you may enjoy making a quilt together. Don't forget whose project it is, however, and ruin the results (and the experience) by trying to make the quilt too perfect. As you can see from Daniel's quilt, Betsy had to adjust the size of each backing rectangle to accommodate Daniel's designs, and we think that this adds a unique, personal, and artistic touch.

Finished Size: 21″ × 32″

Materials

6 solid-color rectangles,
  approximately 8″ × 8½″
fabric scraps in an assortment of
  colors and prints
18″ × 29″ fabric base for front
  background
21½″ × 32½″ fabric backing
22″ × 33″ quilt batting
basic sewing supplies (see page 9)
sewing machine

Procedure

Step 1. Let your child select fabrics and cut shapes such as houses, cars, animals, people, or flowers for each rectangle. Iron all the shapes.

Step 2. Cut eight solid-color rectangles to size, adjusting them if necessary, to accommodate the cut fabric shapes. Let your child place the shapes on the rectangles.

Step 3. Pin the shapes in position and machine zigzag them in place.

Step 4. When all the rectangles are complete, machine appliqué them to the fabric backing using a zigzag stitch.

Step 5. Assemble a quilt sandwich, as described on page 29. Bind the edges by turning the quilt back over the front of the quilt and folding into a hem to form a border all around the quilt. Pin and stitch down.

Step 6 (optional). Quilt each square by any method described in the Quilting section beginning on page 30.

Scotty and Apple Bibs

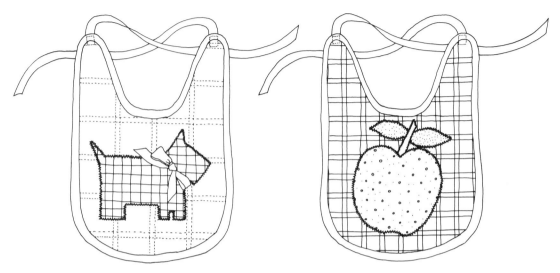

People with young children know that they can never have too many wonderful bibs. We backed ours with quilted fabric because its thick texture keeps most of the food from soaking through and it washes beautifully. Inexpensive and simple to make, these bibs make great gifts.

Although the Scotty and Apple Bibs have different appliqués, their basic construction is the same. Feel free to experiment with other appliqué designs too, such as a cat, house, bear, or any simple shape.

Finished Size: approximately 8½″ × 10½″

Materials

¼ yard quilted fabric
¼ yard (or scraps) gingham for Scotty dog or fabric for apple, stem, and leaves
½ yard plaid ribbon for Scotty dog (optional)
2 yards bias tape
sewing machine
basic sewing supplies (see page 9)

Procedure

Step 1. Enlarge and trace the basic bib pattern onto fabric. Cut it out leaving a ¼-inch seam allowance all around.

Step 2. Enlarge and trace the patterns of either the Scotty dog or the apple onto fabric(s). For machine appliqué, cut the shapes along the drawn line. To complete these bibs with a machine straight stitch or by hand, see the section on Appliqué that begins on page 18.

Step 3. *Scotty Bib.* Pin the dog onto the background right side up. Slip the ribbon under the neck of the dog, center it, and pin it in place. Machine zigzag all around the dog. Remove the pins. Tie the bow around the neck of the dog.

Apple Bib. Pin the leaves in place on the background right side up. Machine zigzag them in place. Pin the stem. Zigzag it in place. Pin the apple. Zigzag it in place.

Step 4. Attach the bias tape around the edges of the bib, following the instructions on the package or using our instructions on page 42.

Step 5. Fold about one yard of bias tape in half vertically and sew it closed with a machine straight stitch. Cut it in equal halves. Attach each half to the top section of the bib, stitching it in place by hand or machine.

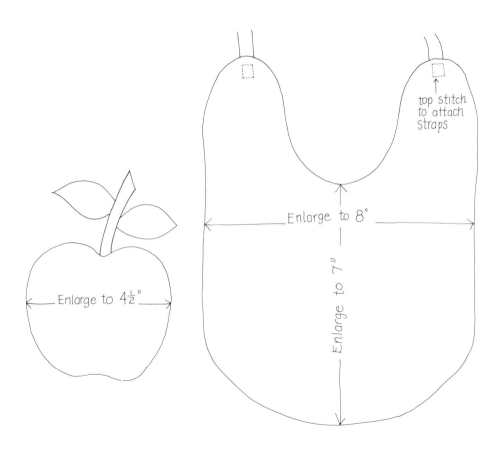

top stitch
to attach
straps

Enlarge to 8"

Enlarge to 7"

Enlarge to 4½"

Scotty Plaid Quilt

Although Betsy's closet is crammed with a rainbow of calico, pindot, and gingham fabrics, when her cat Ginger pulled a scrap of a plaid shirt from the shelves one morning, we were determined to create a project around it. As it turned out, there were only two or three more tiny scraps of plaid tucked away, but we were easily able to find wonderful plaids in local fabric stores.

We spent the afternoon drawing Scotties and deciding on fabric arrangements. During the evening Betsy cut and assembled the quilt top and did the hand quilting over the next two days. The finished quilt is one of our favorite projects in this book, and we're sure that babies will be fascinated with the bright-red plaids. In fact, we liked the end result so much that Betsy went on to make the stuffed Scotty and Scotty Bib that follow.

Finished Size: 28″ × 44″

Materials

½ yard muslin
½ yard plaid (background for front squares)
1½ yards plaid fabric for backing
¼ yard (or scraps) each of eight additional plaids (for Scotties and patchwork strip border)
¼ yard (or scrap) black fabric for black Scotty
4 muslin strips, 2″ × 46″
quilt batting
bias tape—two packages or 4 yards
2½ yards plaid ribbon (¼″ wide) cut into 15 6″ strips (optional)
basic sewing supplies (see page 9)
sewing machine

Procedure

Special note: If you choose to complete this project by hand, be sure to leave a ¼-inch seam allowance around the outside edge of all Scotties when cutting them out. For more on appliqué, see page 18.

Step 1. Cut eight 8″ × 8″ muslin squares and seven 8″ × 8″ plaid squares.

Step 2. Enlarge the Scotty to the size shown in the drawing. Make a template, as described on page 24. Using the template, trace 15 Scotties onto fabric: eight plaid ones, six white or muslin ones, and one black one. Cut them out along the drawn lines.

Step 3. Tie 15 small bows with the plaid ribbon. Hold them against the Scotty to test them for size. Pin each one in place on the necks of the dogs and sew them securely in place with a few hand stitches. Remove the pins.

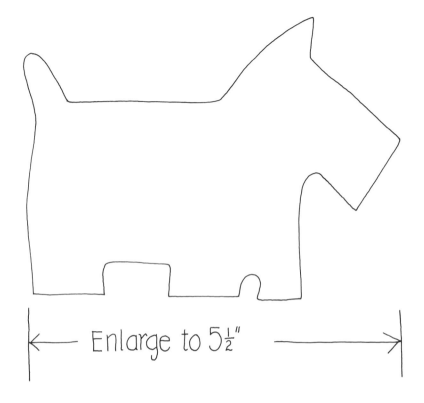

Enlarge to 5½"

Step 4. Center and pin the Scotties onto the squares. The solid-color Scotties go on the plaid squares, and the plaid Scotties go on the muslin or solid-color squares.

Step 5. Machine zigzag the Scotties in place.

Step 6. Iron each square flat.

Step 7. Working on a large flat surface, place the squares in the desired layout and attach them together in three vertical strips, according to the instruc-

tions on page 16 for patchwork. Leave a ¼-inch seam allowance on all sides.

Step 8. Attach the muslin borders around the outside of the quilt top, as described on page 40. First sew the top and bottom borders. Then stitch the side muslin strips in place. Use machine straight stitching and leave a ¼-inch seam on all sides.

Step 9. Using all the plaids, construct the border strip, according to the instructions on page 41.

Step 10. Attach the plaid border strips.

Step 11. Assemble the quilt according to the instructions on page 29.

Step 12. Hand quilt along the inside edge of each square to form vertical and horizontal stitching, according to the instructions on page 30. In addition, hand quilt around the outline of each Scotty. Put in additional quilting through the center of each border strip.

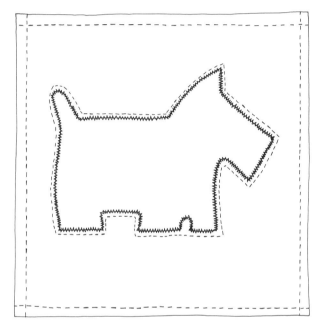

Machine appliquéd Scotty and hand quilting

Scotty Dog

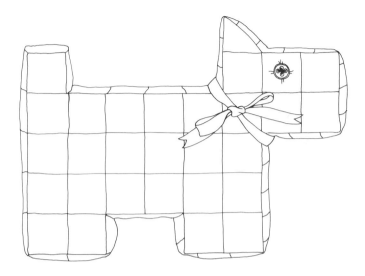

When all our plaid fabrics were piled together, they looked so terrific we couldn't resist making a Scotty Dog. We charted it out on graph paper and the finished toy, which is soft, cuddly, and washable, coordinates beautifully with the Scotty Quilt.

Try our Scotty. We think you'll be happy with him. When you're done, you might want to try charting out other shapes. A house, a cat, a giraffe, or an elephant could be easily adapted to this technique.

Finished Size: 9″ × 12″ (approximately)

Materials

¼ yard each of 5 to 10 different plaid fabrics

2 buttons (about ½″ in diameter) for eyes

½ yard contrasting ribbon for the neck (optional)

stuffing

basic sewing supplies (see page 9)

sewing machine

Procedure

Step 1. Make a patchwork strip border, as described on page 41, consisting of 33 plaid squares that are 2 inches wide.

Step 2. Following the chart with the layout of the dog, cut the strips, as shown. Make two diagonal pieces for the ears by cutting one 2-inch square in half diagonally. Stitch the squares together in row increments, as shown.

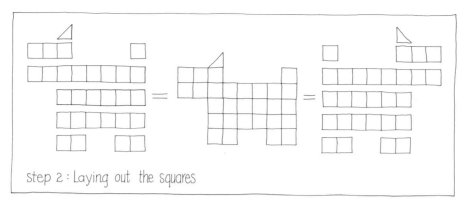

step 2 : Laying out the squares

There are six horizontal rows in all, counting the ear. Repeat this procedure for the back side of the Scotty, making sure that your second Scotty is facing the opposite direction.

Step 3. Using the long strip of 33 squares and starting out at a leg (see the diagram), place the strip and the Scotty front face to face and machine stitch them together with a ¼-inch seam. This boxing technique is also described on page 47.

Pinning is difficult here, and it is simpler at this stage to hold the sides together and ease the corners into place as you go. Sew by machine. The wrong side of the Scotty should be facing up on the machine as you sew.

Go all the way around the Scotty leaving *no* openings. At the end, fold under your last square and hand stitch it so you have a clean seam.

Step 4. Repeat Step 3 with the other side of the Scotty, but this time leave about a 3-inch opening for stuffing.

Step 5. Reverse the Scotty, making sure to poke out all the corners with the point of a pin.

Step 6. Stuff the Scotty firmly.

Step 7. Sew the seam closed, using a hand hem or whip stitch.

Step 8. Place the buttons for the eyes. Sew on both buttons at the same time by going straight through the head of the dog, using a long needle with doubled thread. End off the thread by wrapping it around the button.

Step 9. Tie a ribbon around the Scotty's neck and make a bow.

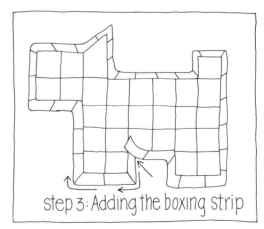

step 3: Adding the boxing strip

The I-Can-Do-It Book

At very early ages, our children loved to look at books, identify the objects, and play with the pages. But most activity books are paper and can be quickly destroyed by young fingers. So we decided to design our own out of more durable materials. While we don't suggest you throw this book into a crib and walk away, we're sure if you sit with your favorite toddler and let him or her turn the pages and play with the pictures, both of you will find pleasure and stimulation. Older children will be able to manipulate the zipper, buttons, snap, and laces that we have built into our book. And with a little thoughtful supervision, we think it will be enjoyed through many playtimes.

Finished Size: 11½″ × 9″

Materials

11½″ × 9″ felt—two pieces each in the following colors: gray-blue, coral, pink, chrome yellow, purple, bright green, dark pink; one piece in the following colors: white, light blue, dark blue, chartreuse, aqua

Special note: Felt precut into approximately 11½″ × 9″ is available in yard goods shops and variety stores in a wide range of colors and qualities. Check a few places to find the best choices.

When you assemble the pieces for the I-Can-Do-It Book, you'll notice that the felt rectangles are cut rather haphazardly. We suggest you set aside all the sheets that are to be the pages of this project and trim them evenly with a straight edge before you begin to appliqué.

gingham scraps—3½″ × 9½″, 1¾″ × 1½″
5″ × 8″ striped cotton
6″ × 6″ solid-color cotton, pale yellow or color of your choice
3″ × 3″ cotton pindot
three 1¾″ buttons
⅜″ × 11½″ rainbow ribbon
6″ heavy-duty plastic zipper
19″ shoelace
½″ snap
pinking shears (optional). In a few places we have trimmed the felt with pinking shears, but this is because we already have them and we love to use them. But we find ourselves using shears less than we hoped when we bought them. Our advice to you is if you have pinking shears, this is the time to use them. If not, don't rush out and buy a pair. The project will work just fine without them.
#5 pearl cotton or 6-strand embroidery floss and needle in brown, bright pink, green, aqua
carbon paper or dressmaker's carbon
basic sewing supplies (see page 9)
sewing machine

Procedure

The I-Can-Do-It Book contains five pages, including the cover, with appliqué shapes. The last and sixth page is blank, although you may want to stitch a design of your own on it or sign it with your name or your child's name. Before beginning this project, we suggest you read the section on appliqué that begins on page 18. Although we chose to use a lot of hand stitching, you may prefer to use machine appliqué.

The Cover: I CAN DO IT

Step 1. Enlarge the design to the size given in the drawing, as described on page 21. Transfer the enlarged design to tracing paper.

Step 2. Iron all materials. Using dressmaker's carbon, trace and transfer all

the shapes onto the wrong side of the fabric. The head, neck, shirt, and handkerchief are cotton. The collar, button placket, and pocket are felt.

Step 3. Cut out the cotton shapes, leaving a ¼-inch seam allowance on all sides. Cut the felt directly on the drawn line since felt needs no hemming. Turn under and baste all cotton hems.

Step 4. Layer all shapes to be appliquéd on the felt backing fabric. Pin or baste them in position. If you use pins, place them so the pins can be removed easily when the stitching is complete. For the cover of the I-Can-Do-It Book, the shapes should be layered in the following order from the bottom up: the striped shirt, the collar and button placket, the pocket, the neck, the head.

Step 5. Hand stitch all the shapes in position, using the whip stitch (page 38). Use a thread color that blends with the shape you are sewing. Remove the pins or basting when you no longer need them or when they get in your way.

Step 6. To do the embroidery, transfer the outlines of the face and letters to the areas to be embroidered using dressmaker's carbon. Or, if you prefer, pin the tracing paper with the drawing of the embroidery directly on the fabric. Embroider through the paper into the fabric. Tear away the paper as you no longer need it. Use the stitches shown in the diagram. Make French knots on the shirt collar and button placket, as shown.

Step 7. Center the rainbow ribbon in the middle of the neck and fasten it with a few backstitches. Tie the ribbon into a bow. Set aside.

Page 1: The Boot

Step 1. Enlarge the boot to the given size, as described on page 21. Transfer the enlarged design to tracing paper.

Step 2. Iron all materials. Using dressmaker's carbon, trace the boot and the cuff onto the wrong side of the felt. Cut out the boot along the drawn lines. If you have pinking shears, use them to cut out the cuff. If not, use straight scissors.

Stitch Guide for the I CAN DO IT BOOK

lettering: back stitches
°° french knots
--- running stitches
ᵒᵒ straight stitches

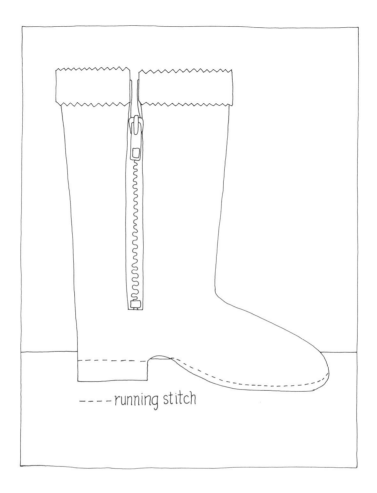

----running stitch

Step 3. Place the closed zipper in the boot opening and machine straight stitch down one side of the opening, across the bottom and up the other side of the boot into the zipper backing. Place the felt cuffs on top of the boot and machine straight stitch them in position, as shown.

Step 4. Cut the gingham fabric to size for the flooring. Turn under the seam allowance and pin it in position on the

felt backing. Appliqué the flooring in place using small whip stitches.

Step 5. Place the boot in position on the backing fabric and floor fabric and pin. Whip stitch it securely in place.

Step 6. Using three strands of embroidery floss or #5 pearl cotton, put in two lines of stitching, as shown, using the running stitch. Set aside.

Page 2: The Shirt

Step 1. Enlarge the shirt to the given size, as described on page 21. Transfer the enlarged design to tracing paper.

Step 2. Iron all materials. Using dressmaker's carbon, trace all the shapes onto the wrong side of the fabric. The shirt body and button placket are felt. The collar and cuffs are cotton.

Step 3. Cut out the cotton shapes leaving a ¼-inch seam allowance on all sides. Cut the felt directly on the drawn lines since felt needs no hemming. Turn under and baste all the hems. Cut three long rectangular shapes (⅛" × 2") for the buttonholes where the buttons are to go.

Step 4. Layer all the shapes to be appliquéd on the felt backing fabric. Pin or baste them in position. Place the

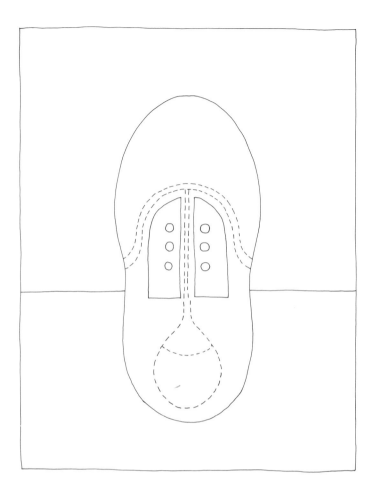

shirt shape down first. Lay the collar and cuffs down next so that they overlap the shirt. Using thread that blends with the fabric, whip stitch all the edges in place.

Step 5. Pin the button placket in position and stitch it down the left side with small whip stitches. Mark the center of each buttonhole with a pen dot. Sew the buttons in place, using the dots as a guide. Set aside.

Page 3: The Sneaker

Step 1. Enlarge the sneaker to the given size, as described on page 21. Transfer the enlarged design to tracing paper.

Step 2. Iron all materials. Using dressmaker's carbon, trace all the shapes on the wrong side of the fabric. All the fabrics in the sneaker are felt.

Step 3. Cut out the felt shapes: the sneaker and four shoelace plackets and the floor, directly on the drawn line. If you are using pinking shears, use them on the top of the floor. If not, use straight scissors. For strength, place two plackets on top of each other and whip stitch them together. Repeat for the second pair of plackets.

Cut three small round holes (¼-inch diameter) in each doubled placket for the lacing. Bind the holes with the buttonhole stitch (see page 38) or leave them plain. (We used grommets for ours, but they aren't holding up well.) Set the plackets aside.

Step 4. Transfer the outlines to be embroidered on the sneaker, using dressmaker's carbon.

Step 5. Place the floor shape in position on the backing fabric, pin and machine stitch it in place on all sides. Next, place the sneaker in position, pin and machine stitch it in position.

Step 6. With four strands of embroidery floss or #5 pearl cotton, use the running stitch to put in the lines of embroidery on the sneaker.

Step 7. Place the plackets in position on the sneaker and whip stitch them along the curved edge and across the bottom. Do not sew down the plackets along the edge that faces the center.

Step 8. Lace the sneaker and set it aside.

Page 4: The Pants

Step 1. Enlarge the pants to the given size, as described on page 21. Transfer the enlarged design to tracing paper.

Step 2. Iron all materials. Using dressmaker's carbon, trace all the shapes onto the wrong side of the fabric. The pants and cuffs and fly are felt. The knee patch is cotton.

Step 3. Cut the felt shapes directly on the drawn lines. Cut the cotton shape leaving a ¼-inch seam allowance on all sides. Turn under and baste the hems.

Step 4. Transfer the outlines to be embroidered on the pants using dressmaker's carbon.

Step 5. Center the pants on the felt backing and pin. Machine straight stitch the pants in position around the outside edge. Pin the cuffs in position on the bottom of each leg. Machine straight stitch. Pin the cotton shape on the knee for the patch and whip stitch it in position.

Step 6. With four strands of embroidery floss or #5 pearl cotton, use the running stitch to put in the lines of embroidery for the pockets, waistband, and fly.

Step 7. Attach the placket for the snap to the front of the pants by whip stitching with matching embroidery floss down the straight side of the placket. Stitch half of the snap in place on the underside of the placket and the

other half on the body of the pants, using hand sewing thread. Add decorative backstitches (page 37) on the top of the placket to outline the snap. Set aside.

Binding

Step 1. Cut four pieces of felt 4″ × 11½″.

Step 2. Arrange each page in a pile in the order that it will appear in the book. Place a blank felt rectangle in a matching color behind each page. Be sure to include a doubled blank felt page for the back cover.

Step 3. Move the pages so the book is open to the center. The shirt page will be facedown on the left. The sneaker page will be faceup on the right. Without changing the position of the pages, sandwich a felt strip between the shirt page and its back (facedown on the left) and the sneaker page and its back (faceup on the right), as shown. Pin the pages securely all around the edges. Remove them from the layout and set them aside.

Step 4. Repeat this procedure with the next two pages in the layout. Sandwich the felt strip between the boot page (facedown on the left) and the pants page (faceup on the right). Pin the pages securely all around the edges. Remove them from the layout and set aside.

Step 5. Repeat this procedure for the cover and back page. Be sure that the cover is facedown on the left.

Step 6. When all the pairs are pinned securely, machine straight stitch around the outside of each page, ¼ inch in from the edge.

Step 7. When the stitching is complete, place all the double pages in final position, opened to the center of the book. Machine straight stitch a line down the center through all three layers of the felt strips to form the spine of the book. Fold the book into the closed position.

Bears Shoe Bag

You can never have too many places to store your baby's or child's things, so you may find yourself using our Bears Shoe Bag for more than just shoes. Dolls, toys, and other small items fit perfectly in the pockets. Six-year-old Jesse Jarnow loves this hanging for storing his favorite tapes and cassettes.

Finished Size: 23″ × 34½″

Materials

23″ × 34½″ quilted cotton, double sided if possible
3½ yards of bias tape in a matching color
12 pieces of 8″ × 8″ solid-color cotton for the pockets
12 pieces of 6″ × 7″ felt for the bears
12 pieces of 2½″ × 3½″ felt for the hearts in two contrasting colors
embroidery floss or thread to match each color of felt
dark embroidery floss and hand sewing needle for bears' faces
three ¾″ plastic rings for hanging the bag (optional)
basic sewing supplies (see page 9)
sewing machine

Procedure

Step 1. Cut the backing fabric to size and attach the bias tape around the outside edge, as described on the package or on page 42.

Step 2. Cut out the 12 pockets to the size shown in the illustration. Turn under the top hem of each and machine zigzag it in position. Set the pockets aside.

Step 3. Enlarge the bears to the dimensions given in the illustration, as described on page 21. Make a template, as described on page 24. Using the template as a guide, outline 12 bears on felt and cut them out along the drawn lines. Repeat this procedure to make 12 bears, six each in two different colors.

Step 4. Pin the bears in the center of each pocket. Hand stitch or machine zigzag them in place in a thread color that blends with the felt.

When the bears are attached, pin a felt heart in the center of each bear and sew it in position using the same technique.

Stitch the bears' faces using French knots and straight stitches, as shown on the chart and described on page 38.

Step 5. Pin the pockets in position on the quilted backing so that the top of the pocket is spread to its full width and the bottom lies flat. The sides should be parallel to the vertical sides of the backing fabric. Machine zigzag each pocket in place leaving the top of each open.

Step 6. Sew the ¾-inch plastic rings along the back top edge for hanging the shoe bag (optional).

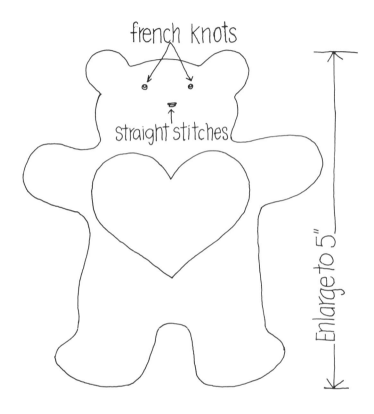

Washcloth Puppets

We always found that our children enjoyed their baths so much more if they had a soft comforting toy to entertain and distract them, so we designed these terrycloth puppets especially for *Welcome Baby.* We made them from velour hand towels and covered them with simple embroidery stitches and soft trimmings. They come together very quickly, and the results are so cheerful that they make wonderful gifts, especially when packed in a basket with mild baby soap.

Washcloth Bear

Finished Size: approximately
9″ × 10″

Materials

11½″ × 10″ beige velour hand towel
#5 pearl cotton in brown, blue, and red
embroidery needle
14″ × ⅞″ ribbon (optional)
waterproof marker or chalk
cardboard
tracing paper
basic sewing supplies (see page 9)
sewing machine

Procedure

Step 1. Enlarge the bear shape given, using the method described on page 21. Make a cardboard template as described on page 24, as well as a tracing paper template with an outline of the face and paws.

Step 2. Fold the towel in half horizontally with velour sides together. Pin securely since terrycloth tends to shift.

Step 3. Place the template on the cloth so that the bottom edge of the template is lined up with the finished bottom edges of the towel. If you are using toweling without a hem, you will have to stitch your own.

Step 4. Trace the bear template onto the terrycloth with a waterproof marker, chalk, or ballpoint pen. Cut out the bear shape using a sharp scissors that can cut through two layers of terrycloth at the same time. Leave a ¼-inch seam allowance on all sides. Remove the pins.

Step 5. Pin the tracing paper onto the velour (front) side of the bear to use as a stitch-placement guide. Make your embroidery stitches right into the paper and terrycloth. Complete your stitches, gently tearing away the paper when it is no longer needed. Make the stitches according to the instructions on page 37.

Step 6. When the embroidery is com-

enlarge to 10"

plete, remove any excess tracing paper. Place the embroidered side of the puppet shape face to face with the velour side of the puppet back. Pin and machine stitch around the outside edge. Begin and end the stitching with a secure backstitch and leave the bot-

tom of the puppet open to insert the hand.

Step 7. When the stitching is complete, remove the pins. Carefully snip into the curves of the seam allowance. Turn the puppet right side out. Push out the ears and paws with a pencil or other blunt instrument.

Step 8 (optional). Pin a soft, washable ribbon around the bottom edge of the puppet, tucking under the raw ends. Hand stitch the ribbon in place along the top and bottom edge.

Washcloth Fish

Finished Size: approximately 11″ × 7½″

Materials

11½″ × 10″ sea-green velour hand towel

#8 pearl cotton in yellow and red embroidery needle
14″ × 1″ satin ribbon in multicolor dots
16″ large pink rickrack
hand sewing thread in pink
waterproof marker or chalk
cardboard
basic sewing supplies (see page 9)
sewing machine

Procedure

Step 1. Enlarge the fish shape given, using the method described on page 21. Make a cardboard template, as described on page 24.

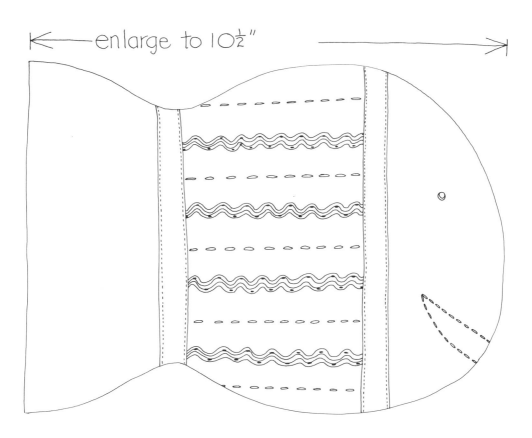

enlarge to 10½″

Step 2. Fold the towel in half horizontally with the velour sides together. Pin it securely as terrycloth tends to shift.

Step 3. Place the fish template on the terrycloth so that the tail of the fish is lined up with the finished edge of the towel. If you are using toweling without a hem, you will have to stitch your own.

Step 4. Trace the fish template onto the terrycloth with a waterproof marker, chalk, or ballpoint pen. Cut out the fish shape using a sharp scissors that can cut through two layers of terrycloth at the same time. Leave a ¼-inch seam allowance on all sides. Remove the pins.

Step 5. Choose one half to be the face of the fish. Cut the ribbon and rickrack to size and pin it in place on the velour side of this piece, as shown in the illustration (page 123). Layer the ribbon *over* the rickrack to seal off its raw ends.

Sew the rickrack in place by putting a tiny running stitch in each point. Sew the ribbon in place with hand-running stitches along each edge or with machine stitching.

Step 6. Put in the embroidery as shown, using the stitch guide on page 37.

Step 7. When the stitching is complete, place the embroidered appliquéd side of the fish face to face with the velour side of the fish back. Pin them securely and machine stitch around the outside edges. Begin and end the stitching with a secure backstitch. Leave the bottom of the puppet open for inserting a hand.

Step 8. When the stitching is complete, remove the pins. Carefully clip the curves of the seam allowance. Turn the puppet right side out. Push out the curves with your hand, if needed.

Animal Hangers

We remember buying for our babies and being given as gifts irresistible articles of clothing that wouldn't fit for years. It always seemed like such a shame to tuck away that fabulous sweater or incredible pair of overalls in a drawer. Occasionally, we ended up hanging whatever it happened to be on the wall as a room decoration. It was inconceivable to us at the time that our babies would ever be big enough to wear a size 2 or 3.

But the metal hangers seemed so unappealing, and when we saw fabric-covered hangers in a baby shop, we couldn't resist buying them. We added felt animal faces for a quick and easy project that is just the right touch in any baby's room.

Finished Size: hanger—
   approximately 12″ wide
cat face 4″ × 4″; rabbit face 4″ × 5″

Materials (for one hanger)
1 covered fabric hanger 12″ long,
   available in baby stores and closet
   shops
9″ × 12″ felt rectangle
scraps of felt in four additional colors
hand sewing needle and thread
6-strand embroidery floss in three
   colors

embroidery needle
20″ × ¾″ ribbon
polyester fiberfill
pinking shears (optional)
basic sewing supplies (see page 9)
sewing machine

Procedure

Step 1. Trace the cat or rabbit and cut
out the pattern as described on page
23. They are shown here in actual size.

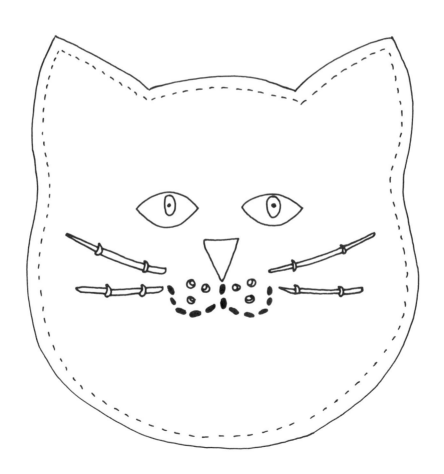

Step 2. Iron all materials. Fold the felt in half and pin it securely. Place the paper pattern onto it and trace. Cut out two felt shapes along the drawn lines. You need not leave a seam allowance. Use pinking shears if you have them.

Step 3. Using a whip stitch and hand sewing thread, sew the felt pieces for

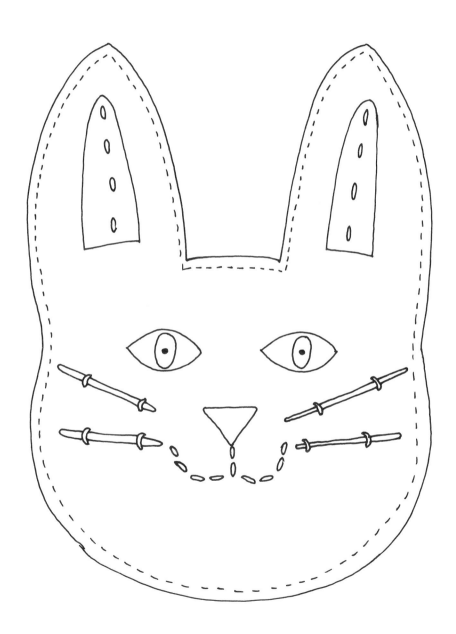

the eyes and other features to the face of the animal, using the drawing to guide your placement.

Step 4. Using the drawing as a guide, do the embroidery.

Step 5. Place the embroidered face *faceup* with the backing piece so they are aligned. Machine straight stitch ⅛ inch from the edge around the entire outside of the animal shape.

Step 6. Make a small incision in the felt backing and insert small amounts of the polyester fiberfill until the shape is filled. Hand stitch to close the incision. Attach the felt face to the front of the hanger with hidden but secure whip stitches through the back of the felt into the fabric hanger.

Step 7. Tie a bow and attach it to the neck, using the same technique.

Catch-all Basket

When a baby is squirming on the changing table and it's hard to hold him or her down, it's great to have all the paraphernalia you need right at hand. It's easy to reach if it's organized in our great-looking catch-all basket. When Daniel was born 13 years ago, Betsy had an ugly plastic container to hold powder, pins, and wipes. She wishes she had realized how easy it would have been to make this project.

Consider making this basket in other sizes, smaller or larger, for gifts or for favors at showers and other parties.

Finished Size: approximately 9″ diameter, 5″ deep plus basket handle

Materials

½ yard printed fabric

2 yards gathered eyelet lace
(1″ wide)

large rubber band or 12″ thin elastic

2 yards ribbon (to match printed
fabric)

wicker basket with handle (from 9″
to 15″ diameter)

quilt batting (5 strips 4″ wide and
44″ long)

silk flower for decoration (optional)

glue or paste (optional)

basic sewing supplies (see page 9)

sewing machine (optional)

Procedure

Step 1. Cut the fabric in a circle 1½ inches larger than the measurements of the basket (see the diagram). We used the lid of a pot for our circle, but a compass is even better.

Step 2. Baste or pin the eyelet lace to the wrong side of the circle all the way around. The inner edge of the lace should overlap the fabric about ¼ inch, and the ruffled edge should stick out beyond the fabric at least ¾ of an inch. Sew the eyelet in place using hand sewing, machine straight stitch, or machine zigzag.

Step 3. Using the batting strips, wind the batting around the sides of the basket two or three times until all the batting is used up, or until the basket is as puffy as you would like it to be.

Step 4. Lay out the fabric circle on a flat surface with the right side down.

Catch all basket

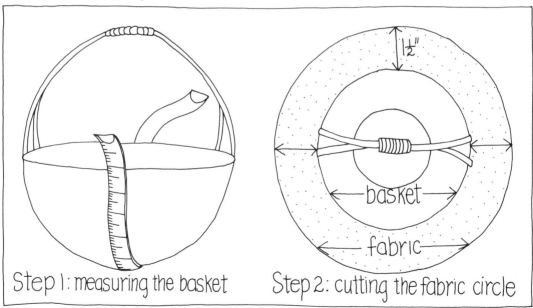

Step 1: measuring the basket

Step 2: cutting the fabric circle

Place the basket with the batting wrapped around it in the center of the fabric. Gather the fabric around the sides of the basket and fasten it with a rubber band or elastic so that the elastic stays on the line between the basket and the lace. Redistribute the fabric to make the gathers even all around the basket.

Step 5. Wrap the ribbon around the basket to cover the elastic and tie an attractive bow.

Step 6 (optional). Insert silk flowers into the bow.

Step 7 (optional). If the lace is floppy and will not stand up neatly, you might want to glue or paste it to the rim of the basket in a few places.

Baby Carrying Basket

This is truly a grandmother's project because it is made with such attention to detail. Ann Gardiner lined this basket and made accessories for her grandson, and it is a work of art.

When Ann saw a newborn baby being carried in a lined basket, she was captivated. When she saw a finished basket for sale in a children's shop, the amount on the price tag convinced her to make her own. She made the lining, the quilt, and the pillow in the evenings during the course of a week, sewing much of the trim and seam binding by hand because she preferred the elegance of hand stitching.

This is one of the most spectacular projects in *Welcome Baby*. It takes no longer to make than any of the other projects, but the materials are the most costly. However, whatever you spend to do-it-yourself, expect the finished basket to cost at least twice as much (and be not nearly half as nice) in a baby boutique.

Finished Size: (approximate)

The basket: 30″ × 20″, 11″ deep
The quilt: 26″ × 34″
The pillow: 8″ × 12½″

Where to Get the Basket:

Basket shops and garden shops often carry baskets large and sturdy enough for a baby. Ann was able to find one with two strong fabric straps already attached. Baskets are also available through the mail from Basketville, R.R. 1, Putney, Vermont 05346.

Materials for the Lined Basket

a basket with a flat bottom,
    approximately 22″ × 15″
3 yards of quilted cotton fabric
10 yards of bias tape
8 yards of ⅜″ satin ribbon
8 yards of lace, approximately 2½″
    wide
8 yards of 2″ wide gathered ruffle in
    the same print as the quilted
    cotton
tape measure
18″ × 24″ lightweight paper
basic sewing supplies (see page 9)
sewing machine

Procedure

Since baskets come in varying shapes and sizes, we can't be sure that your basket will match our model exactly. We have outlined the procedure in the following section, but we want you to be ready to adjust the measurement to your needs. Ann designed the lining to fill the basket gently, rather than to fit snugly, so don't panic if you don't have a perfect fit. This looseness will allow you to remove the lining easily for laundering.

Step 1. Fit a sheet of lightweight paper against the bottom of the basket and trace the shape of the oval bottom onto it. Trim away the paper so that only the oval remains. Using the paper as a pattern, trace the oval onto the wrong side of the quilted fabric. Cut out the oval leaving a ¼-inch seam allowance on all sides.

Step 2. Cut the remaining fabric into a 12″ × 85″ strip, or a size appropriate to your basket. For a basket of different dimensions, make sure the strip is long enough to circle the inside of the basket with several inches left for the seam allowance. The strip should also be deep enough to overlap the lip of the basket by 1 inch plus the seam allowance.

Step 3. Place the fabric oval in the bottom of the basket, facedown. Lay the fabric strip around the inside of the basket, also facedown. You will have to ease the fabric into position because of the sloping sides of the basket. Pin the fabric overlap, right sides together. Remove the lining from the basket and machine straight stitch it shut.

Step 4. With right sides together, fit the bottom edge of the strip around the outside of the oval along the drawn line and pin. Machine stitch them together. Remove the pins.

Step 5. Turn the lining right side out and fit it into the basket. Determine the position of the handles on each side. Mark the outside extremities with pins. With a sharp scissors, cut a line in the lining for the handles to come through approximately 2 inches from the top edge of the fabric, as shown.

Step 6. Following the directions on the package, or those given on page 42, finish off the edges of each strap hole with bias tape in a color that matches the lining fabric.

Step 7. Attach bias tape around the top outside edge of the lining and (optional) over all the raw seams.

Step 8. Replace the lining in the basket faceup. Pin one or two rows of lace and trimming, as desired, around the top edge of the lining so it can curve over and cover the top lip of the basket. Machine stitch the lace and trimming in place. For a finished look, pin the ⅜-inch wide ribbon over the line of machine stitching and hand stitch it in place.

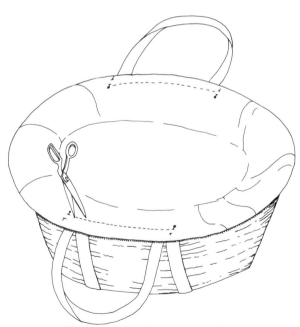

Step 5: Cutting lines for the handles

Step 9. Place the lining in the basket in a faceup position and draw the handles through their openings. Tie two 8-inch ribbons next to each handle, as shown. Tie bows to help keep the lining in place.

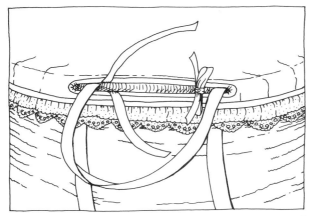

Step 9: Stitching and tying ribbons to the lining.

The Baby Carrying Basket Quilt

Finished size: 26″ × 34″ plus lace

Materials for the Quilt

26″ × 34″ quilted cotton in the
   same print as the lining
3½ yards bias tape
3½ yards 2″ wide lace to match the
   lace on the lining
18″ of ⅜″ wide satin ribbon
   (optional)
basic sewing supplies (see page 9)
sewing machine

Procedure

Step 1. Trim the fabric to size and finish all the edges with bias tape, as described on the package and on page 42.

Step 2. Pin the lace around the top edge of the quilt just below the bias tape and machine stitch it in position.

Step 3. Tie a small bow with the ⅜-inch wide satin ribbon and hand stitch it to one corner of the quilt (optional).

The Baby Carrying Basket Pillow

Finished size: 8″ × 12½″

Materials for the Pillow

2 pieces of quilted cotton in the same print as the lining, measuring 8″ × 12½″ each

3½ yards of 2″ wide lace to match the lace on the lining
3½ yards of coordinated ruffle trim (optional)
12″ × ⅜″ wide satin ribbon (optional)
polyester fiberfill
basic sewing supplies (see page 9)
sewing machine

Procedure

Step 1. Cut two pieces of quilted cotton to 8″ × 12½″ plus the seam allowance.

Step 2. Pin the ribbon and any other desired trim around the outside edge of the face of the fabric, as shown in the illustration. If you are using lace, pin it securely so that the ruffled edge will not be caught in the seam when you sew it.

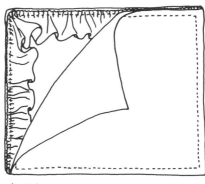

Adding ruffles

Step 3. Pin the pillow front and back together face to face and machine stitch them on all sides. Leave a 3-inch opening on the bottom edge for reversing the pillow.

Step 4. Carefully turn the pillow right side out and remove all the pins.

Step 5. Fill the pillow with polyester fiberfill until you reach the desired density. Hand stitch shut the open seam. For more on pillow construction, see page 45.

Baby Sleeping Pillow

When Betsy's children were little and napping, she hung a sign similar to this one on their doors. It asked others politely to keep their voices down and not to go barging into the room. As we were writing this book, Betsy confessed that she sometimes put it on the door when she was napping also.

Although counted cross-stitch may look complicated, it takes very little time to learn. It also works up very quickly and is a good television or take-along project.

Finished Size: 5½″ × 6¾″, including fabric borders

Materials

¼ yard Aida cloth (light blue, if possible)
6-strand embroidery floss: white, black, green, yellow, brown, blue, pink
embroidery needle
⅛ yard solid-color fabric for border
⅛ yard printed fabric for border
¼ yard printed fabric for pillow back
1 yard gathered eyelet lace
¼ yard narrow ribbon to hang pillow
stuffing
basic sewing supplies (see page 9)

Procedure

Step 1. Following the chart given, make the cross-stitch top. See the section on counted cross-stitch on page 34.

Step 2. When the top is completed, cut the Aida cloth leaving eight extra rows on all sides around the stitchery. Iron it flat.

Step 3. Cut the solid fabric into four strips that are 1 inch wide and 10 inches long. Attach the top and bottom strips according to the instructions for fabric borders on page 40. When the stitching is complete, cut the edges of the solid fabric to match up with the Aida cloth. Iron them flat. Repeat for all four sides of the sampler. Iron everything flat.

Step 4. Cut strips of printed fabric 3 inches wide and 14 inches long. Attach the printed fabric borders following the same technique. Iron everything again.

Step 5. Pin the eyelet lace onto the right side of the sampler with the edges together and the eyelet facing inward. Place the pins perpendicular to the edge of the sampler and work carefully around the corners.

Pin ¼-yard loop of narrow ribbon into the center of the top edge on top of the eyelet. Attach the ribbon using a machine straight stitch leaving a ¼-inch seam.

Step 6. Cut the backing fabric to the same size as the top.

Step 7. Leave the lace pinned in place and pin the backing fabric face to face with the sampler. Beginning on the bottom edge, machine straight stitch around the pillow, ⅛ inch in from the row of stitching that is holding the lace in place. Include all corners in your stitching, but leave about 4 inches open at the bottom to reverse and stuff the pillow.

Step 8. Turn the pillow right side out. Work carefully to avoid pricking yourself. Remove the pins.

Step 9. Stuff the pillow, making sure to get the stuffing into the corners and along the edges.

Step 10. Close up the seam by hand, using either the hem or whip stitch.

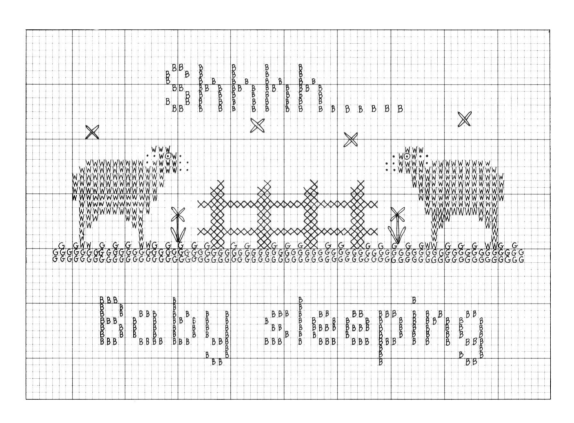

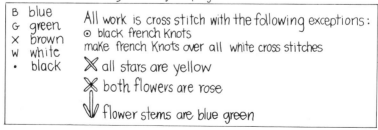

Color and Stitch Key for Baby Sleeping Pillow

B	blue	All work is cross stitch with the following exceptions:
G	green	⊙ black french knots
X	brown	make french knots over all white cross stitches
W	white	✕ all stars are yellow
•	black	✕ both flowers are rose
		⬇ flower stems are blue green

Welcome Baby Pincushion

This is another of our favorite projects because it represents the joint efforts of several friends. Super calligrapher Jackie Fisher designed the lettering. It was cross-stitched by the authors, and Lani Hee constructed the final product by turning it into a pincushion basket. A good place to keep extra diaper pins or safety pins, it can also be used as decoration in the baby's room, and it makes a terrific shower gift.

If you are a first-time cross-stitcher, don't be intimidated. It's a lot of fun. Cross-stitch instructions are on page 34.

Finished Size: 7¼″ by 8″, including basket

Materials

white Aida cloth (about 10″ × 10″)
embroidery floss—pink, blue, and green or colors of your choice
¼ yard (or scraps) of solid fabric to frame sampler
scraps to make outer border on sampler (about five to ten different fabrics)
1 yard gathered white eyelet lace
glue

wicker basket (When you go to the store to get the basket, bring along your completed needlework with its fabric strip borders. The needlework must fit right into the top of the basket.)
stuffing
panty hose or nylon stocking
large rubber band

Procedure

Step 1. Following the chart shown, stitch the sampler. See page 35 for further instructions on counted cross-stitch.

Step 2. Trim the sampler leaving 1 inch on all sides beyond the stitched border.

Step 3. Cut the solid fabric into four 1″ × 10″ strips. Attach the strips to the sampler, as described on page 40, Fabric Borders.

Step 4. Construction of patchwork border: Cut five to ten 1″ × 12″ strips of scrap fabrics. Following instructions on page 41, assemble patchwork strip.

Step 5. Cut the completed patchwork strips into appropriate lengths and attach them as a second border around the outside edge of the needlework following the same procedure.

Step 6. Cut four strips of about 3″ × 14″ in any fabric. These strips will never show in the finished product,

but you will need them to tuck in the sides when you construct the basket. Sew the strips onto the four sides of the cross-stitch panel.

Step 7. Iron the cross-stitch panel with the borders.

Step 8. Fill the panty hose or stocking with enough stuffing to fill the basket in the desired shape.

Step 9. After stuffing, close up the panty hose with a knot.

Step 10. Place the cross-stitch panel on top of the stuffing and draw a rubber band around the whole thing. Arrange the shape on top to the desired smoothness. This step may sound a little strange, but it works very well and the shape is easy to control.

Step 11. Put glue in the bottom and lower sides of the basket.

Step 12. Place the stuffing inside of the basket rim, leaving room around the top for the eyelet.

Step 13. Measure the inside of the basket rim and cut the eyelet to size allowing enough length for it to overlap itself slightly.

Step 14. Put glue on the inside of the basket rim and insert the eyelet lace. Distribute the lace evenly. Use a long pointed object to redistribute the lace between the basket and the stuffing.

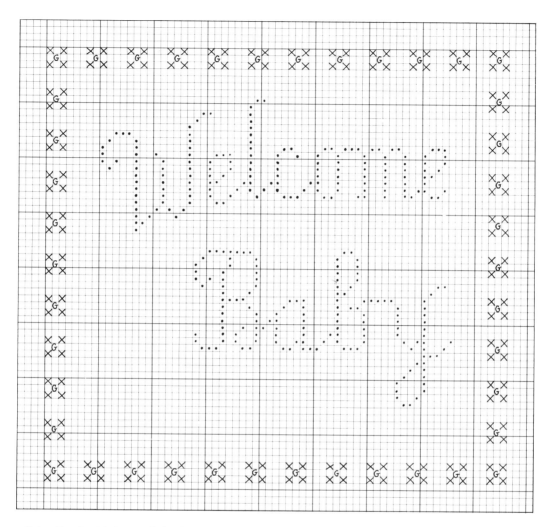

Color Key for Welcome Baby Pin Cushion

✕	pink
G	green
•	blue

Bibliography

de Dillmont, Thérèse. *Encyclopedia of Needlework*. Mulhouse, France: Editions Thérèse de Dillmont, 1979.

Hopkins, Mary Ellen. *The It's Okay If You Sit on My Quilt Book*. Atlanta: Yours Truly, Inc., 1982.

Ickis, Marguerite. *The Standard Book of Quiltmaking and Collecting*. New York: Dover Publications, 1959.

Jarnow, Jill. *The Patchwork Point of View*. New York: Simon and Schuster, 1975.

————. *The Complete Book of Pillow Stitchery*. New York: Simon and Schuster, 1979.

————. *Sampler Stitchery*. Garden City, New York: Doubleday and Co., 1982.

Leman, Bonnie, and Judy Martin. *Log Cabin Quilts*. Denver: Moon Over the Mountain Publishing Co., 1980.

Puckett, Marjorie, and Gail Giberson. *Primarily Patchwork*. Redlands, California: Cabin Craft, 1975.

Ryan, Mildred Graves. *The Complete Encyclopedia of Stitchery*. Garden City, New York: Doubleday and Co., 1979.

Thomas, Mary. *Mary Thomas' Embroidery Book*. New York: Gramercy Publishing Co., reprint from 1936.

Wien, Carol Anne. *The Great American Log Cabin Quilt Book*. New York: E. P. Dutton, 1984.